Religion AND *Society*

VICTOR W. WATTON

Hodder & Stoughton

A MEMBER OF THE HODDER HEADLINE GROUP

ACKNOWLEDGEMENTS

The publishers would like to thank the following for permission to reproduce material in this book:

BUAV for the extract from a recent publication; Christian Education Movement for extracts from *What the Churches Say on Moral Issues*, reproduced by permission; T & T Clark for extracts from *The Third Reich and the Christian Churches* by P Matheson; Continuum Publishing for extracts from *The Catechism of the Catholic Church*; HarperCollins Publishers for extract from *Hope and Suffering* by Desmond Tutu; Muslim Educational Trust for extracts from *What Does Islam Say?* by Ibraham Hewitt; Oxford University Press for the extracts from *The Upanishads* translated by Patrick Olivelle (Oxford World's Classics, 1998) © Patrick Olivelle (1998), by permission of Oxford University Press; Pax Christi, USA for various extracts; Penguin UK for the extract from *Hinduism* by K M Sen (1961), reproduced by permission of Penguin Books; Polity Press for extract from *Sociology* by A Giddens; Transworld Publishers © Space Time Publications Ltd 1988. Extracted from *A Brief History of Time* by Stephen Hawking, published by Bantam Press, a division of Transworld Publishers. All rights reserved; SPCK for the extract from *Science and Creation* by J Polkinghorne; Quotations from the English translation of *The Catechism of the Catholic Church for Australia* © 1994 St Pauls, Strathfield, Australia/Libreria Editrice Vaticana, used with permission.

Scriptures quoted from The Holy Bible, New International Version by Hodder & Stoughton © 1973, 1978, 1984 International Bible Society, with permission; The Holy Qur'an, translated by Yusuf Ali © IPCI, with permission.

The publishers would like to thank the following individuals, institutions and companies for permission to reproduce photographs and illustrations in this book:

Achinto/Christian Aid/Still Pictures p42; AKG Photo London (Andre Normil) p120; Bridgeman Art Library pp16, 22, 65, 115; Circa Photo Library (Zbignieu Kosc) p12, (William Holtby) p14; Corbis pp44 (Joe McDonald), 45 (Frank Lane Picture Agency), 46 (John Periam, Cordaiy Photo Library Ltd), 47, 48 (Richard T Nowitz), 49 (David H Wells), 51 (Angelo Hornak), 54 (Humphrey Evans), 56, 60, 100, 103, 104, 109 (Reuters NewMedia Inc, 57 (David Rubinger), 67 (Ted Spiegel), 68 (Tiziana and Gianni Baldizzone), 70 (Flip Schulke), 76 (Bettman), 79 (David Reed), 83 (Eldad Rafaeli), 84, 85 (Hulton-Deutsche Collection), 97 (Stephanie Maze), 118 Gary Braasch, 119 (Kevin Schafer); Mark Edwards/Still Pictures pp36, 40; Eye Ubiquitous p10; Jewish National Fund p43; PA News p17, 18, 20, 21, 23, 27, 31, 52, 63, 71, 78, 81, 82, 86, 87, 88, 99, 106, 110, 111; David Rose p8; Peter Sanders p66; Science Photo Library (Martin Dohrn) p98, (Mehau Kulyk) 121, (David A Hardy) 123.
With thanks to Jill Watton for supplying photographs (pg 8, 24, 25, 26, 30, 32, 33, 35, 38, 72, 73, 80, 96).

Every effort has been made to trace and acknowledge copyright. The publishers will be happy to include details of copyright holders it has not been possible to contact in subsequent editions.

Dedication
For my children and grandchildren – Simon, Rebecca, Timothy, Abigail, Peter, Benjamin and Kisa.

Orders: please contact Bookpoint Ltd, 130 Milton Park, Abingdon, Oxon OX14 4SB. Telephone: (44) 01235 827720, Fax: (44) 01235 400454. Lines are open from 9.00–6.00, Monday to Saturday, with a 24 hour message answering service. Email address: orders@bookpoint.co.uk

British Library Cataloguing in Publication Data
A catalogue record for this title is available from The British Library

ISBN 0 340 799676

First published 2001
Impression number   10   9   8   7   6   5   4   3   2
Year   2006   2005   2004   2003   2002   2001

Copyright © 2001 Victor W. Watton

Cover photo from Photodisk.
Typeset by Liz Rowe
Printed in Italy for Hodder & Stoughton Educational, a division of Hodder Headline Plc, 338 Euston Road, London NW1 3BH by Printer Trento

CONTENTS

Chapter 4 Religion: Crime and Punishment 70

Chapter 5 Religion and Medical Issues 94

Chapter 6 Religion and Science

PREFACE

This book has been written for the new Edexcel GCSE Religious Studies Specification A. In conjunction with the *Teacher's Handbook*, also published by Hodder and Stoughton, it provides a complete resource for those preparing for the Edexcel Specification A Unit H, Religion and Society.

It provides resources on Christianity, Islam, Judaism and Hinduism which are colour coded by religion. Those wishing to study Buddhism or Sikhism alongside Christianity for Edexcel Specification A Unit H will find it helpful to use *Buddhism – A New Approach* or *Sikhism – A New Approach* in conjunction with this book. These are also published by Hodder and Stoughton.

There is no criticism of the religious attitudes covered in this book. This is to encourage students to think and evaluate for themselves. However, the *Teacher's Handbook* has photocopiable sheets of alternative viewpoints as well as revision files on every topic in Edexcel Unit H.

The word God is used throughout rather than using Allah in Islam and the Almighty in Judaism. This is to ensure that non-Muslim and non-Jewish students are not led into thinking that Jews or Muslims worship a different God.

When dates are given, the letters CE and BCE are used. These stand for Common Era and Before the Common Era, as AD and BC imply belief in Christianity.

I hope that students and teachers will find the book both useful and enjoyable and become more thinking and tolerant citizens as a result of their studies.

INTRODUCTION

Most of you will have studied Christianity, and probably the other religion you are offering for GCSE, up to Key Stage 3, but here is a reminder of some background facts about these religions which will be essential for your GCSE course:

CHRISTIANITY

Basic Christian beliefs

- Christians believe that there is only one God, who acts in the world as Father, Son and Holy Spirit (the TRINITY).

- They believe that God created the world and humans in his image. God is love, and out of love, he sent his son to live and die for humanity.

- Many Christians believe that Jesus died to save people from the punishment which human sin deserves – death. They believe that if people believe in Jesus as God's son and their saviour, they will have eternal life in heaven.

- Christians believe that the Bible is the word of God. Although they have different opinions about exactly what this means, they all believe that the Bible tells the truth about Jesus and contains the Christian teachings about God and how life should be lived.

How Christians make moral decisions

- All Christians believe that moral decisions should be based on the teachings of Jesus in the New Testament and the Ten Commandments in the Old Testament.

- ROMAN CATHOLICS believe that these teachings are best interpreted by the Church, especially the Head of the Church – the Pope. So, to make moral decisions, they would refer to the teachings of the Church contained in *The Catechism of the Catholic Church* (1994) or encyclicals (long letters containing the Pope's teachings) published by the Pope.

- ORTHODOX CHRISTIANS would base their decisions on how the Bible has been interpreted by councils of bishops, or simply ask advice from their priest (many Catholics would also do this).

- PROTESTANTS (Church of England, Methodist, Baptist, Pentecostal etc.) believe that each individual should make their own decision on the basis of what the Bible says, but most would also be guided by decisions made by

Factfiles concerning Christian beliefs and ideas are colour coded like this:

democratically elected bodies of Church leaders (e.g. the General Synod of the Church of England or the Conference of the Methodist Church).

Orthodox, Roman Catholic and some Evangelicals do not allow women priests, other Christians do.

Roman Catholics do not allow contraception, other Christians do.

Charismatics and many Evangelicals believe it is right to try to convert members of other religions, other Christians do not.

Catholic and Evangelical Christians believe homosexuality is condemned by God, other Christians do not.

Why there may be differences of opinion among Christians

- Christianity developed in different places in different ways. By the time Christianity became the official religion of the Roman Empire in 356 CE, there were several different traditions within Christianity. In the West, the Bishop of Rome (the Pope) became accepted as leader among the bishops in that part of the Empire. The Eastern Churches (Orthodox) were ruled by councils of bishops. By 1054, the Eastern and Western branches of the Church had divided from one another.

- In the sixteenth century, men like Martin Luther and John Calvin accused the Western Church of going a long way from the Church of the New Testament. They protested and demanded reforms (the Reformation). This led to the Protestant or Reformed Churches which believed in the Church being ruled democratically (they taught that all Christian believers are priests and therefore equal with each other) and in the absolute authority of the Bible.

More recently, some Protestant Christians decided that there was too much interpretation of the Bible without accepting the Bible as the absolute word of God. These Evangelical Christians emphasise the need for conversion (being born again by accepting Jesus Christ as your saviour) and for accepting the Bible as the words of God. They are sometimes known as fundamentalists because they want to go back to the fundamentals (basics) of the Christian religion.

All Christian Churches have also been influenced by the Charismatic Movement which emphasises the need for Christians to be filled with the Holy Spirit and consult God directly, through the Holy Spirit, when needing advice. Charismatic Christians practise spiritual healing and speaking in tongues.

- Differences of opinion among Christians may therefore arise because of:
  - the way they understand the authority of the Church;
  - the way they interpret the Bible;
  - the importance they place on the Holy Spirit;
  - the importance they place on their own personal experience.

Shared ministry is one way Churches are coming together.

ISLAM

Muslims always refer to God as Allah because this is the Arabic word used for God in the Qur'an. However, in this book, the word God is used so that non-Muslims do not think Muslims are worshipping a different god.

Basic Muslim beliefs

- Islam means submission to God's will which brings peace to the world. Muslims believe Islam was the original religion given by God to Adam, the first man and first prophet.

- Muslims believe there is only one God who made the world and humans to act in unity with him and with each other. God's oneness is so important that the worst sin for a Muslim is to associate other beings or things with God (so Muslims cannot worship pop stars or football heroes).

- Muslims believe that Muhammad was given God's absolute and final word (the QUR'AN), directly by God and that, because it was written down immediately in the way God wanted, there will never be a need for another prophet.

- Muhammad established Islam not only as a religion, but also as a community (ummah) with all its laws based on the teachings of the Qur'an.

- Muslims believe that the purpose of life is to worship God. They follow God's laws as God revealed them to Muhammad and practise the five Pillars of belief, prayer, giving to the poor, fasting in Ramadan and going on pilgrimage to Mecca (Makkah). If all this is done, then, after death, they will go to heaven for eternity.

Factfiles concerning Muslim beliefs and ideas are colour coded like this:

How Muslims make moral decisions

- Because Islam began as a community religion, there has always been an Islamic legal system based on God's laws. This is known as the SHARI'AH (the way God wants men to walk). The Shari'ah is based mainly on God's words in the Qur'an, though it also uses the Sunnah (examples and sayings of Muhammad as recorded in hadith). Muslims believe that Muhammad was the final prophet sent by God and so what Muhammad said and did is the final example for humans on how to live their lives.

- So when Muslims make moral decisions, they find out what the Shari'ah says. If this does not cover the particular point, then they will ask a Muslim lawyer for advice (Muslim lawyers are also religious leaders) or read the Qur'an to see if that gives a relevant teaching.

- Everything Muslims are allowed to do is called HALAL and everything they are forbidden to do is called HARAM.

Examples:

Some Muslim Law Schools say eating shellfish is wrong, others say it is allowed.

Shi'ah Muslims allow men to have a temporary marriage, Sunnis do not.

Some Muslims say it is wrong to watch TV programmes showing the sexes mixing and women in non-islamic clothes, others say it is all right as long as they are not doing evil things.

Why there may be differences of opinion among Muslims

- When the Shari'ah was being sorted out, there were some differences of opinion between Muslim scholars and four law schools were established (Hanifite, Hanbalite, Malikite, Shafi'ite) and Muslim lawyers belong to one of these schools. Each Muslim country follows the Shari'ah as set down by one of these schools and so there are bound to be some differences.

- Most Muslims (85 per cent) are Sunni (follow only the sunnah of Muhammad). However, some are Shi'ah who also follow the hadith of Ali (Muhammad's cousin and son-in-law) and the teachings of Muhammad's descendants through Ali. The Shi'ah are therefore bound to have some differences of opinion from the Sunni.

- The Shari'ah dates to the Prophet Muhammad but was not formalised until 900 CE, so it has no rulings on things like TV. Lawyers have to work out laws on these, and lawyers can disagree.

- Some Muslims think there should be one state of Islam joining all Muslim countries together. Others think there should be separate Muslim countries like Pakistan and Saudi Arabia.

The Holy Ka'aba, the centre of Islam.

JUDAISM

Jews always refer to God as The Almighty, because they think God's name is too holy to be used. However, in this book, the word God is used so that non-Jews do not think Jews are worshipping a different god.

Basic Jewish beliefs

- Jews believe that there is only one God who is righteous and good and who is to be worshipped by following his moral commands (ETHICAL MONOTHEISM).

- They believe that God created the world and humans. They believe that God chose people like Adam and Noah to tell the world about him and to keep true religion. Then God chose Abraham and made a special COVENANT with Abraham that he would give Abraham and his descendants the land of Canaan and make a great nation of his descendants as long as Abraham and his descendants kept God's laws.

- They believe that God made a covenant with the Jews through Abraham and Moses. As part of the covenant made with Moses, God gave the Torah, God's commandments, so that by following it, the Jews could be God's holy nation and bring the rest of the world to true worship of God.

- Jews believe that if they try to keep all God's commandments, then their names will be recorded in the book of life.

- The Jewish holy book is the TENAKH (the same as the Protestant Christian Old Testament). It is in three parts: TORAH (the 'laws' given to Moses), NEVIIM (the 'prophets' including the historical writings) and KETUVIM (the 'writings' e.g. Psalms).

Factfiles concerning Jewish beliefs and ideas are colour coded like this:

How Jews make moral decisions

- Jews believe that there are commandments of God (MITZVOT) for every situation in life. These are found in the Torah and are explained in the TALMUD, a collection of Jewish teachings which dates from about 500 CE.

- Where it is difficult to decide what these mitzvot mean for today, Jews rely on rabbis who are expert in the Torah and Talmud, and on the decisions of great rabbis in the past. These decisions form the basis of detailed guidelines for how to live life as a Jew and are called HALAKHAH (path).

- Every country with a sizeable Jewish population has a Bet Din made up of the best qualified and most respected rabbis who make decisions for the Jews of their country on new moral issues and on matters like divorce.

- Jews are therefore totally dependent on God's commandments for making moral decisions.

Examples:

Some Jews (mainly Hasidic) believe Israel should not have been founded until the Messiah arrived.

Reform, Liberal and many Orthodox Jews believe Jews can wear whatever clothes they like, as long as men cover their heads, but the Hasidic and some Orthodox believe Jews must wear special clothes.

Reform and Liberal Jews give men and women equal divorce rights; Orthodox and Hasidic only allow divorce if the husband agrees.

Reform and Liberal Jews allow women to sit with men in the synagogues, Orthodox and Hasidic do not.

Why there may be differences of opinion among Jews

- For nearly two thousand years there was no homeland or centre for Judaism, so different interpretations arose in different areas. In particular the Jews living in the Muslim Empire (now called Sephardi Jews) and those living in Europe (called Ashkenazi Jews) developed different interpretations and even developed different popular forms of the Hebrew language.

- In the seventeenth and eighteenth centuries there was argument among European Jews about the need for joy and closeness to God. Hasidic Judaism developed from this debate.

- In the nineteenth century there were calls to modernise Judaism. The Orthodox (who include Sephardi, Ashkenazi and Hasidic Jews) said Jews had to obey all God's commands literally, but two new groups, Reform Jews and Liberal Jews, said that the Law needed to be interpreted, so that Judaism could adapt to the needs of the modern world.

Orthodox Jews praying at the Western Wall of the Temple of Jerusalem.

HINDUISM

Basic Hindu beliefs

- The name Hinduism is a word used by Westerners to refer to the native religions of India, but it is better to speak of Hinduisms because there is no one religion with a set of clear beliefs.

- There are many different forms of Hinduism. Some Hindus worship several gods, some worship only one. Generally Hindus tend to believe that there is a universal soul (Brahman) which is revealed in the various gods and goddesses of Hinduism and in the soul of every living creature.

- Hindus regard the Vedas, Upanishads, Gita and Ramayana as holy books, but they do not think of them in the same way that Jews, Muslims or Christians think of their scriptures. Hindus are guided by them, but do not think of them as the word of God.

- Hindus believe that life is like a wheel – people are born, they live, they die, they are re-born (reincarnation). Life is governed by the law of cause and effect (KARMA) and the purpose of life is to achieve liberation (MOKSHA) from the wheel of life and the law of karma.

- What people are re-born as depends on their actions. Everyone is set a path of actions (DHARMA) which, if fulfilled, will lead to salvation.

- The ideas of karma and dharma have influenced the caste system where what people are born as is determined by their previous existence and they must do their dharma in that caste if they are to achieve salvation.

Factfiles concerning Hindu beliefs and ideas are colour coded like this:

How Hindus make moral decisions

- Tradition lays down what is the dharma for each caste. Every Hindu is supposed to follow four stages of life (ashramas). The first of these is the student ashrama, when Hindu children are taught the dharma for their caste. These traditions are taught and/or interpreted by brahmins (priests) and are based on Hindu law codes such as the Code of Manu (they are not based on the scriptures).

- When new situations arise, Hindus tend to rely on the teachings of the gurus or swamis (teachers or spiritual leaders) who lead their Hindu sect.

- Some Hindus act as their own guru and make moral decisions based on what they think Hinduism is.

Why there may be differences of opinion among Hindus

- There are bound to be different practices in Hinduism, because there are so many different forms of Hinduism and new groups are appearing all the time. For example, the temple in Neasden is the work of the Swaminarayan Hindu Mission. Other Hindu sects in Britain include Hare Krishna (Iskcon), Sai Baba and Rama Krishna Vedenta Mission.

Examples:

Some Hindus are vegetarian, others eat meat (but not beef).

Some Hindus refuse to drink alcohol, others believe it is a gift from God.

Some Hindus believe in the caste system, others (like the Swaminarayan) have rejected the caste system.

Some Hindus think they ought to marry to fulfil their householder ashrama, others think they can by-pass this stage and dedicate themselves to God instead of marrying.

Dedicated to God at Varanasi on the holy River Ganges.

Differences and similarities between religions

Although there are differences within and between religions, the differences can be exaggerated. As can be seen in the issues covered in this book, some Christians, Muslims, Jews and Hindus agree more with each other on an issue than with fellow members of their own religion.

Not all members of a religion have the same ideas. An Orthodox Jew may refuse to use a car to go to synagogue, but have liberal attitudes on the status of women. A Catholic Christian may attend a Catholic church, but have Protestant views on contraception.

People are individuals and so, although general statements can be made about the beliefs and attitudes of a religion, there will always be individual members of the religion who do not fit the statement.

NON-RELIGIOUS PEOPLE AND MORAL ISSUES

It is often thought that people need religion to behave in a moral way, but non-religious people can be very moral people, just as some religious people can be immoral.

Non-religious people use one or more of the following ideas when making moral decisions:

• Some look at what the law says. For example, if they were thinking about whether to give euthanasia to someone they loved, they would look at the law and not use euthanasia because the law bans it.

• Some look at the consequences of an action. They ask themselves what the results would be of the different choices they could make. Often they are guided by which result will bring the greatest happiness or the least misery to the most people (this is known in philosophy as Utilitarianism). For example, if looking at the issue of abortion, they would look to see whether banning abortions would bring greater happiness and less misery than allowing them. If they thought it would, they would not have an abortion.

• Some use the idea that because people have to live with each other in the world, they should use their instinct to guide them to what is right and then work out what it would be like if everyone did what their instinct is telling them. For example, if their instinct told them it was right to have an abortion, they would then work out what the world would be like if everyone in their situation had an abortion. If they decided it would make the world a better place, then they would have the abortion.

LABOUR'S NEW SLEAZE

BOTH RELIGIOUS AND NON-RELIGIOUS PEOPLE ARGUE ABOUT THE MORALITY OF POLITICIANS

① RELIGION AND SOCIAL RESPONSIBILITY

FACTFILE 1

HOW CHRISTIANS MAKE MORAL DECISIONS

BIBLE – THE HOLY BOOK OF CHRISTIANS WITH **66** BOOKS SPLIT INTO THE OLD TESTAMENT AND THE NEW TESTAMENT.

CHURCH – THE COMMUNITY OF CHRISTIANS (WITH A SMALL C, IT MEANS A CHRISTIAN PLACE OF WORSHIP).

CONSCIENCE – AN INNER FEELING OF THE RIGHTNESS OR WRONGNESS OF AN ACTION.

SITUATION ETHICS – THE IDEA THAT CHRISTIANS SHOULD BASE MORAL DECISIONS ON WHAT IS THE MOST LOVING THING TO DO IN A SITUATION.

ELECTORAL SYSTEM – THE WAY IN WHICH VOTING IS ORGANISED.

FIRST-PAST-THE-POST – THE VOTING SYSTEM WHERE WHOEVER GETS THE MOST VOTES IN A CONSTITUENCY (AREA REPRESENTED BY AN MP) WINS THE SEAT.

PROPORTIONAL REPRESENTATION – THE VOTING SYSTEM WHERE SEATS ARE DISTRIBUTED ACCORDING TO THE PROPORTION OF VOTES EACH PARTY GETS.

NATIONAL GOVERNMENT – THE GOVERNMENT HEADED BY THE PRIME MINISTER WHICH GOVERNS THE WHOLE COUNTRY.

LOCAL GOVERNMENT – THE LOCAL COUNCIL WHICH LOOKS AFTER LOCAL ISSUES SUCH AS EDUCATION AND REFUSE COLLECTION.

DECALOGUE – THE TEN COMMANDMENTS

GOLDEN RULE – THE TEACHING OF JESUS THAT PEOPLE SHOULD TREAT OTHERS AS THEY WOULD LIKE TO BE TREATED.

The doctrinal standards of the Methodist Church are based upon the Divine revelation recorded in the Holy Scriptures which revelation Methodism acknowledges as the supreme rule of faith and practice.

From *What the Churches Say* second edition.

God is the author of Sacred Scripture because he has inspired its human authors; he acts in them and by means of them. He thus gives assurance that their writings teach without error his saving truth.

Catechism of the Catholic Church.

The Lindisfarne Gospels (698 CE) are the earliest copy of the Bible produced in England.

Christians base their moral decisions on three things:

1 The Authority of the Bible

The authority of the Bible means that the Bible is accepted as being so important that what it says must be believed and obeyed. All Christians agree that the Bible has authority because it is inspired by God. All Christians would use the Bible as a basis for making moral decisions – for example if deciding whether it is right to steal, they would refer to the Ten Commandments which state that it is always wrong to steal and decide not to do it. The Bible has many teachings on how to make moral decisions and how Christians ought to behave. Most important are the Decalogue and the teachings of Jesus in such things as the Sermon on the Mount.

However, there are differences among Christians about the authority of the Bible:

- Some Christians believe that the Bible is the absolute word of God dictated by God to the writers. Therefore it has absolute authority and can never be changed.

- Some Christians believe that although the Bible is the absolute word of God, it needs interpreting by the Church.

- Other Christians believe that the Bible was written by humans inspired by God, so that, although it has authority for moral decision making, many of its attitudes reflect the social situation at the time of the writers (for example St Paul's attitude to women and slaves) and need to be revised in the light of modern knowledge.

2 The authority of the Church

Although the Bible is the basis of all Christian decision making, most Christians believe that the Bible needs to be explained for life today. Most Christians believe that the Church has the right to explain what the Bible means, and what Christians should do about moral issues.

The Bible contains a whole set of stories, experiences, prayers and poems which reflect a pattern of God's dealings with a line of people that he got in touch with. Through these patterns we can come to know how God makes himself known, but I do not hold that the Bible is the word of God in any sense that guarantees its particular words.

David Jenkins, former Bishop of Durham, quoted in *Christians in Britain Today* D. Cush.

The General Synod is the 'parliament' of the Church of England. It contains 560 members and consists of three 'houses' of Bishops, Clergy and Laity, who meet together twice a year ... When preparing to make statements upon moral issues, the specialist department, or Board, will be asked to produce a theological rationale as guidance in the decision-making process. The most relevant department for moral and social issues is the Board for Social Responsibility. When motions are finally passed, a distinction will often need to be made between a principle laid down by the General Synod and its practical application, which will need to take account of individual circumstances.

From *What the Churches Say* second edition.

The General Synod makes recommendations on moral issues for members of the Church of England.

Some Churches (for example the Church of England and the Methodist Church) elect people to an Assembly which comes to an agreement about how members of the Church should respond to a moral issue. In the Roman Catholic Church, the Pope and the Council of Bishops act as the Magisterium (the living teaching office of the Church) to give teaching on moral issues to Catholic Christians either through the Catholic Catechism or official letters from the Pope called encyclicals.

Most Christians believe that God did not stop speaking to people after the last book of the Bible was written. They believe that God speaks to the world today through the Church.

The Pope has the final responsibility for stating Roman Catholic views on moral issues.

The Roman Pontiff and the bishops, as authentic teachers, preach to the People of God the faith which is to be believed and applied in moral life. It is also incumbent on them to pronounce on moral questions that fall within the natural law and reason. The infallibility of the *Magisterium* of the Pastors extends to all the elements of doctrine, including the moral doctrine, without which the saving truths of the faith cannot be preserved, expounded or observed.

Catechism of the Catholic Church.

3 The role of conscience

All humans have a conscience which distinguishes between right and wrong and makes them feel guilty if they do things which they regard as wrong. St Paul and St Thomas Aquinas taught that Christians should use their conscience as the final part of moral decision making. A Christian should look at what the Bible and the Church say about a moral issue, but if they feel 'pangs of conscience' about doing it, they should follow their conscience.

A good example would be if a Christian heard the voice of God telling them to kill all doctors who perform abortions. The Bible and the Church say that Christians should obey the voice of God, but they also say that it is wrong to murder. To decide which teaching to follow, a Christian would use their conscience which would tell them that murder is wrong and that Christians should never use wrong means, whatever the end is – although the purpose of stopping abortions may be a good one, that does not justify killing people to achieve it.

Christians should never act against their conscience, which is why Christian soldiers have to refuse to obey orders if those orders mean doing something which their conscience says is wrong.

Some Christians only use the Bible for making moral decisions, some only use the teachings of the Church, some only use the Bible/Church if their conscience agrees with it. Many of those Christians who believe that conscience is more important than the Bible or the Church believe that Christians should follow their conscience whatever the Bible or Church say.

Situation Ethics

This is a Christian idea about making moral decisions which began with an American Christian thinker, Joseph Fletcher.

Accepting the authority of either the Bible or the Church means that things are either right or wrong regardless of the situation. For example, if the Bible says stealing is wrong, it cannot be allowed even if a madman buys nuclear weapons. If the Church says abortion is wrong, it cannot be allowed even if a 12-year old girl is made pregnant as a result of rape.

Fletcher felt that this was wrong and that Christians should base their moral decisions on Jesus' commandment to love your neighbour as yourself and on the situation. So Fletcher said that Christians should only follow the Bible and/or the Church if it is the most loving thing to do. Therefore a Christian would work out that the most loving thing to do in the situation of the madman would be to steal the nuclear weapons from him. The most loving thing to do in the situation of the 12-year-old girl would be to give her an abortion.

A human being must always obey the certain judgement of his conscience. If he were deliberately to act against it, he would condemn himself. Yet it can happen that moral conscience remains in ignorance and makes erroneous judgements about acts to be performed or already committed … A good and pure conscience is enlightened by true faith, for charity proceeds at the same time from a pure heart and a good conscience and sincere faith.

Catechism of the Catholic Church.

Pray for us. We are sure that we have a clear conscience and desire to live honourably in every way.

Hebrews 13:18

There is a principle of reflection in men by which they distinguish between approval and disapproval of their own actions … this principle in man … is conscience.

Sermon 1 – Bishop Butler (quoted in *Dictionary of Christian Ethics*).

One of the teachers of the law came and heard them debating. Noticing that Jesus had given them a good answer, he asked him, 'Of all the commandments, which is the most important?'

'The most important one,' answered Jesus, 'is this: "Hear O Israel, the Lord our God, the Lord is one. Love the Lord your God with your heart and with all your soul and with all your mind and with all your strength." The second is this: "Love your neighbour as yourself." There is no commandment greater than these.'

Mark 12: 28–31

THE ELECTORAL SYSTEM IN THE UNITED KINGDOM

The Cabinet is made up of the Prime Minister and the Ministers in charge of the main government departments and makes major government decisions.

The United Kingdom has two basic layers of government:

National Government is led by the Prime Minister and the Cabinet and must have a majority in the House of Commons. The National Government is responsible for all the areas shown in the pie charts. It is known as 'the Government' and runs the Civil Service and the Armed Forces. It raises money through income tax, VAT etc.

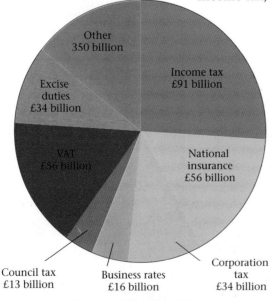

Tax income for the UK 1999–2000.

- Other 350 billion
- Income tax £91 billion
- Excise duties £34 billion
- VAT £56 billion
- National insurance £56 billion
- Council tax £13 billion
- Business rates £16 billion
- Corporation tax £34 billion

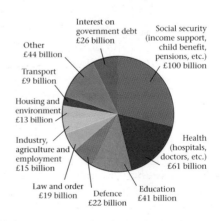

Tax expenditure for the UK 1999–2000.

- Interest on government debt £26 billion
- Social security (income support, child benefit, pensions, etc.) £100 billion
- Other £44 billion
- Transport £9 billion
- Housing and environment £13 billion
- Industry, agriculture and employment £15 billion
- Health (hospitals, doctors, etc.) £61 billion
- Law and order £19 billion
- Defence £22 billion
- Education £41 billion

Local Government is the local council led by the mayor. Councils are responsible for refuse disposal, street cleaning etc. and for administering education, the police force and the fire brigade on behalf of the National Government which provides most of the funding though every householder has to pay tax based on the value of the property.

There are some variations to this. Some areas have two or even three layers of local government with county council, then district council, then parish council each responsible for increasingly local matters. Scotland, Wales and Northern Ireland have their own regional assemblies with a first minister and a cabinet responsible for a variety of matters at regional level. There are also 74 MEPs who represent the United Kingdom in the European Parliament.

How MPs and Councillors are elected

MPs and councillors are elected by the **first-past-the-post system**. Each MP has a constituency with about 65,000 voters. Each councillor has a ward with about 6,000 voters. Electors put a cross next to the name of their preferred candidate, and the candidate who gains the most votes is elected even though they may not have a majority of the votes cast (e.g. the Labour candidate gains 20,000, the Conservative 15,000, the Liberal Democrat 10,000, so the Labour candidate becomes the MP even though more people voted against than for). This system means that a small area is served by an MP or councillor who represents the interests of the area and can be contacted easily by residents (all MPs and councillors hold surgeries in their area when people can go to see them for help with problems).

Ken Livingstone, the Mayor of London, was the first directly elected mayor in England.

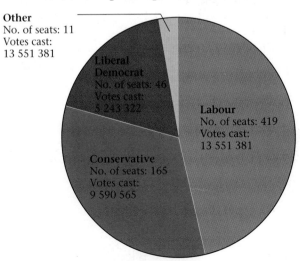

Other
No. of seats: 11
Votes cast:
13 551 381

Liberal Democrat
No. of seats: 46
Votes cast:
5 243 322

Labour
No. of seats: 419
Votes cast:
13 551 381

Conservative
No. of seats: 165
Votes cast:
9 590 565

Votes and seats in the 1997 election.

MEPs and Scottish and Welsh Assembly members are elected by **proportional representation** so that the number of members per party is a more accurate reflection of the proportion of votes cast for them. However, this has the drawback of meaning that the constituencies have to be much larger and it is more difficult for the member to be involved locally.

CHRISTIAN BELIEF IN THE SEPARATION OF RELIGION AND POLITICS

Some Christians believe that religion is concerned with an individual's spiritual development, not with society. They believe that the New Testament teaches that Christians will be judged on how they love God and love their neighbour, not on their politics. Therefore, Christianity is concerned with worship and relationships with individuals whereas politics is concerned with how society should be governed and should work according to political, not Christian, principles.

They believe this because:

- when Jesus was asked whether it was lawful for Jews to pay taxes to the Romans, he said that there is a religious part of life and a political part which should be kept separate. So Christians today should keep their religion separate from their politics (see Mark 12:13-17);

- in Romans and Titus, St Paul said that Christians should obey political leaders because they have God's authority. This means that God looks after politics and Christians have to look after their own souls;

- Church leaders from Martin Luther to the Pope have said that Christians should obey the leaders of the state. In established Churches such as the Church of England and the Lutheran Churches in Sweden and Norway the Church leaders have always been the spiritual advisers to the government, not the political advisers;

- in a multi-faith society, religion must be kept separate from politics, otherwise there is likely to be religious conflict.

> 'Is it right to pay taxes to Caesar or not? Should we pay or shouldn't we?' But Jesus...asked, 'Bring me a denarius and let me look at it.' They brought the coin, and he asked them, 'Whose portrait is this? And whose inscription?'
>
> 'Caesar's,' they replied.
>
> Then Jesus said to them, 'Give to Caesar's what is Caesar's and to God what is God's.'

Mark 12:14–17

> Everyone must submit himself to the governing authorities, for there is no authority except that which God has established. The authorities that exist have been established by God.

Romans 13:1

> Remind the people to be subject to rulers and authorities, to be obedient, to be ready to do whatever is good.

Titus 3:1

Jesus being asked about taxes.

> A Christian is a perfectly free lord of all, subject to none. A Christian is a perfectly dutiful servant of all, subject to all.

The Freedom of a Christian Man Martin Luther (1520).

> In preaching, catechising and religious instruction, as well as in the activities of Catholic organisations and private conversations, anything which could be construed as criticism of the leading personalities in state and community or of the political views they represent should be avoided.

Statement by the Archbishop of Freiburg in June 1933 after the Nazis had come to power in Germany.

Christians formed the Jubilee 2000 group to persuade the governments of rich countries to cancel the debts of poor countries.

Some Christians believe that Christianity is a whole way of life and that it is impossible to separate Christianity from politics. They feel that Christians should decide who to vote for and which political party to work for on the basis of Christian principles.

They believe this because:

- Jesus showed that religion is more important than politics when he threw the money changers out of the Temple;

- in the Sermon on the Mount, Jesus showed that it is impossible to serve God and money, meaning that religion must control politics. If people try to separate religion from politics, they end up being controlled by politics instead of by God;

- the Letter of James shows that religious faith must reveal itself in actions. In just the same way that it is useless to tell someone who is starving to be filled, but do nothing to feed them, so it is impossible for someone to say they believe in God if they do nothing to show it. As politics is the way of changing people's situations, it follows that Christians must be involved in politics;

- the Churches have all made statements about how Christians should be involved in helping the suffering, working for peace, working for a fairer sharing of the earth's resources etc. As all of these require Christians to be involved in politics, it follows that Christians should be involved in politics.

> We are Christian not only in church on Sunday. Our Christianity is not something we put on, like our Sunday best, only for Sunday. It is for every day. We are Christians from Monday to Monday. We have no off day … It is not either worship or trying to do all the good works in our community. It is both.

Hope and Suffering, Desmond Tutu.

CHRISTIAN BELIEF IN INVOLVEMENT IN POLITICS

> **No one can serve two masters. Either he will hate the one and love the other, or he will be devoted to the one and despise the other. You cannot serve both God and money.**

Matthew 6:24

> **What good is it, my brothers, if a man claims to have faith but has no deeds? Can his faith save him? Suppose a brother or sister is without clothes and daily food. If one of you says to him, 'Go I wish you well; keep warm and well fed,' but does nothing about his physical needs, what good is it? In the same way, faith by itself, if not accompanied by action, is dead.**

James 2:14–17

> Socio-economic problems can be resolved only with the help of all the forms of solidarity: solidarity of the poor among themselves, between rich and poor, of workers among themselves, between employers and employees in a business, solidarity among nations and peoples. International solidarity is a requirement of the moral order; world peace depends in part on this.

Catechism of the Catholic Church.

THE WELFARE STATE

The Welfare State as we know it began during the Second World War, though it had its origins in various campaigns against poverty in the nineteenth century and the Liberal Government Reforms of 1906–10 which introduced the first old age pensions in the UK.

The National Health Service provides free hospital treatment for everyone.

During the Second World War, the Government appointed a committee under Sir William Beveridge (a Liberal) to investigate the problems of social insurance. This committee produced the Beveridge Report in 1942. The Report said that there were five evil giants facing Britain which had to be destroyed:

- **Want** many people were living in poverty through no fault of their own because they were sick, widowed, unemployed.

- **Disease** although the Liberals had introduced some medical insurance, there was no free medical treatment and many people could not afford to see a doctor when they were ill.

- **Ignorance** secondary education was only available to those who could pay or who passed a scholarship at the age of 11. Most children left school at the end of elementary education at the age of 14.

- **Squalor** although council housing had been introduced at the end of the nineteenth century, there was not enough and many people were still living in slums.

- **Idleness** – at the start of the war over ten per cent of the workforce was unemployed.

During the war there was a coalition government (all the political parties working together to win the war) which began the Welfare State with the 1944 Education Act. This introduced secondary education for everyone and raised the school leaving age to 15. However, it was the Labour Government of 1945–51 which established the full Welfare State to remove all five of the giants. Want was attacked by the National Insurance and National Assistance Acts. Disease was attacked by the establishment of the National Health Service. Squalor was attacked by a massive council house building programme and the New Towns Act which enabled the setting up of new towns in the countryside for people removed from the knocked down slums of the big cities. Idleness was attacked by the government nationalising some industries and setting up boards to help industries in areas of high unemployment.

The Welfare State today

The Welfare State in the United Kingdom uses National Insurance and taxes to provide:

- free education for everyone up to the age of 18, and help with university education for the poor;

- free doctors and hospitals for everyone and help with prescriptions, dentistry and glasses; payments for people too ill to work;

- payments for the unemployed;

- social security so that everyone has a minimum income;

- pensions for old people;

- child benefit for children under 19 in full-time education;

- housing benefit and housing associations;

- job centres and help for setting up businesses.

> A welfare state exists where government organisations provide material benefits for those who are unable to support themselves adequately through paid employment – the unemployed, the sick, the disabled and the elderly ... All Western countries today have extensive welfare provisions. On the other hand, in many of the poorer countries of the world these benefits are virtually non-existent.

Sociology, A Giddens.

The Welfare State provides training so that everyone can find work.

THE CHRISTIAN BASIS OF THE WELFARE STATE

Most of the reformers and politicians who worked to establish the Welfare State were Christians who were inspired by Christian principles.

The Decalogue (the Ten Commandments in Exodus 20) comprises four commands on relations with God and six on relations with other people:

Relations with God	Relations with other people
Worship one God only	Honour your parents
Do not worship idols	Do not murder
Do not swear using God's name	Do not steal
Keep the Sabbath day holy	Do not commit adultery
	Do not give false evidence
	Do not covet other people's belongings

These commandments make Christians think about the needs of others. Can aged parents be honoured if they do not have pensions? Isn't refusing healthcare to the poor the same as murdering them? Isn't refusing help to the poor and unemployed the same as stealing from them?

Jesus said that **the Golden Rule** of the Christian life is to treat other people as you would want them to treat you. Many Christians feel that this means that those who are rich or in work should pay taxes so that the Welfare State can treat everyone in the way the rich like to be treated.

The Golden Rule

So in everything, do to others what you would have them do to you, for this sums up the Law and the prophets.

Matthew 7:12

Many state schools were founded by Christian Churches who are often still involved in the way they are run.

In the Parable of the Sheep and the Goats, Jesus showed that it is the duty of Christians to feed the hungry, clothe the naked, give drink to the thirsty, visit the sick, help those in prison. The only way in which these things can be done systematically in a Christian country is through something like the Welfare State.

The Christian Church has always felt it has a duty to: educate children so that they can learn about God; help the sick; look after orphans; look after the homeless. Consequently many schools, hospitals and orphanages in the United Kingdom were founded and run by the Christian Church.

Donald Soper was a leading Methodist minister.

The Parable of the Sheep and the Goats

When the Son of Man comes in his glory, and all the angels with him, he will sit on his throne in heavenly glory. All the nations will be gathered before him, and he will separate the people one from another as a shepherd separates the sheep from the goats. He will put the sheep on his right and the goats on his left.

Then the King will say to those on his right, 'Come, you who are blessed by my Father; take your inheritance, the kingdom prepared for you since the creation of the world. For I was hungry and you gave me something to eat, I was thirsty and you gave me something to drink, I was a stranger and you invited me in, I needed clothes and you clothed me, I was sick and you looked after me, I was in prison and you came to visit me.'

Then the righteous will answer him, 'Lord, when did we see you hungry and feed you, or thirsty and give you something to drink? When did we see you a stranger and invite you in, or needing clothes and clothe you? When did we see you sick or in prison and visit you?'

The King will reply, 'I tell you the truth, whatever you did for the least of these brothers of mine, you did for me.'

Then he will say to those on his left, 'Depart from me, you who are cursed, into the eternal fire prepared for the devil and his angels. For I was hungry and you gave me nothing to eat, I was thirsty and you gave me nothing to drink, I was a stranger and you did not invite me in, I needed clothes and you did not clothe me, I was sick and in prison and you did not look after me.'

They also will answer, 'Lord, when did I see you hungry or thirsty or a stranger or needing clothes or sick or in prison, and did not help you?'

He will reply, 'I tell you the truth, whatever you did not do for one of the least of these, you did not do for me.'

Matthew 25:37–40

'I thank God for the Welfare State,' declared Donald Soper in his presidential address to the Methodist Conference in July 1953.

Quoted in *A History of English Christianity*, A Hastings.

Economic activity, especially the activity of a market economy, cannot be conducted in an institutional, juridical or political vacuum. On the contrary, it presupposes sure guarantees of individual freedom and private property as well as a stable economy and efficient public services.

Catechism of the Catholic Church.

QUESTIONS

Factfile 1 How Christians make moral decisions

1 Give an outline of one way in which a Christian would make a moral decision.

2 Explain why the Bible is important to Christians in making moral decisions.

3 'Your conscience is the best guide for deciding what is right and what is wrong.' Give two arguments for and two arguments against this statement.

Factfile 2 The electoral system in the United Kingdom

1 What is the difference between national and local government?

2 What is meant by the first-past-the-post voting system?

3 Have a class discussion on why it is important to vote in elections.

Factfile 3 Christian belief in the separation of religion and politics and 4 Christian belief in involvement in politics

1 Give three reasons why some people think Christianity should be kept out of politics.

2 Give three reasons why some people think Christianity should be involved in politics.

3 'All Christians should be involved in politics.'
Do you agree? Give reasons for your opinion, showing that you have considered another point of view. You should refer to Christianity in your answer.

Factfile 5 The Welfare State

1 Name three features of the British Welfare State.

2 Explain why the Welfare State was set up in the United Kingdom.

3 Have a class discussion on whether it is important to have a welfare state.

Factfile 6 The Christian basis of the Welfare State

1 Write out the main points in the Parable of the Sheep and the Goats.

2 Have a class discussion on whether Christians should support the Welfare State.

3 'Christians should not use private hospitals.' Do you agree? Give reasons for your opinion, showing that you have considered another point of view. You should refer to Christianity in your answer.

② RELIGION AND THE ENVIRONMENT

POLLUTION – THE CONTAMINATION/DEGRADATION OF THE ENVIRONMENT.

GREENHOUSE EFFECT – THE TRAPPING OF CARBON DIOXIDE IN THE ATMOSPHERE, WHICH IS THOUGHT TO INCREASE THE EARTH'S TEMPERATURE.

ACID RAIN – POLLUTANTS SUCH AS COAL SMOKE RELEASE SULPHURIC AND NITRIC ACID, WHICH MAKE RAIN MORE ACIDIC.

NATURAL RESOURCES – NATURALLY OCCURRING MATERIALS, SUCH AS OIL AND FERTILE LAND, WHICH CAN BE USED BY HUMANS.

CREATION – THE ACT OF CREATING THE UNIVERSE, OR THE UNIVERSE WHICH HAS BEEN CREATED.

STEWARDSHIP – LOOKING AFTER SOMETHING SO THAT IT CAN BE PASSED ON TO THE NEXT GENERATION.

ENVIRONMENT – THE SURROUNDINGS IN WHICH PLANTS AND ANIMALS LIVE AND WHICH THEY DEPEND ON TO CONTINUE LIVING.

CONSERVATION – PROTECTING AND PRESERVING NATURAL RESOURCES AND THE ENVIRONMENT.

ANIMAL RIGHTS – THE BELIEF THAT ANIMALS HAVE RIGHTS WHICH SHOULD NOT BE EXPLOITED BY HUMANS.

Scientists often speak of the earth as an ecosystem. By this they mean that the plants, animals and atmosphere of the earth interact with each other to produce all the materials which are needed for life on earth to continue. The problem with an ecosystem is that it is very finely balanced and so altering one of the components can have great effects on the rest of the system (you may have heard of the chaos theory where the fluttering of an extra butterfly in Brazil results in a hurricane in Florida). The changes humans have made to the earth's ecosystem (environment) may cause similar problems. The main problems of pollution are:

THE DANGERS OF POLLUTION

• **The Greenhouse Effect**
The burning of fossil fuels (gas, coal and oil) produces carbon dioxide. This produces a barrier in the atmosphere rather like the glass in a greenhouse so that the heat from the sun can get through, but cannot get back out again. Many scientists believe that this is causing the earth to warm up. This is often called 'global warming'.

A report published by the UK Climate Impacts Programme in October 1998 predicts that the amount of carbon dioxide in the atmosphere will increase by 50 per cent by 2050. This would lead to average temperatures in the south-east of England rising by 1.3 degrees Celsius by 2020 and by 2 degrees Celsius by 2050. There would be rainfall increase of 15–20 per cent in the north of England and Scotland by 2050. Other scientists have claimed that such increases in temperature will lead to a rise in the level of the sea (because of the ice-caps melting) which means some coastal areas could disappear.

• Acid Rain

The burning of fossil fuels such as coal and oil releases sulphuric and nitric acid as well as contributing to the greenhouse effect. These pollutants go into the atmosphere and change the pH of the rainwater in clouds from pH5/6 to pH 3 making it so acidic that it can burn things when it comes to earth. Buildings and forests in countries such as Sweden and Germany are being destroyed by the acid rain produced by the United Kingdom's burning of fossil fuels.

• Eutrophication

An excess of nitrates, nitrites and phosphates in rivers is leading to a lack of oxygen and an increase in aquatic plants which is causing fish to die and poisons to enter water supplies. This is caused by: fertilisers being washed into streams; sewage pollution and a lack of trees to soak up the nitrogen. This could lead to major health problems for humans.

Nuclear power stations, such as this one at Hartlepool, could help to reduce the greenhouse effect.

Some people think the floods of autumn 2000 were a sign of the likely effects of global warming.

• Deforestation

Many scientists are also worried about the way the number of trees on earth is declining. Trees are essential for three things: in the process of photosynthesis they remove carbon dioxide from the atmosphere and put back oxygen; in the nitrogen cycle, they soak up nitrates etc. from the soil; they prevent soil erosion and desertification (fertile land becoming a desert). Scientists fear that if humans go on cutting down trees (almost half the Amazonian Jungle has now been destroyed) major problems will be caused for the environment.

• Radioactive pollution

Nuclear power stations do not produce carbon dioxide, but do produce nuclear waste which will take thousands if not millions of years to be safe. This waste is being buried and no one knows whether the containers it is buried in will be able to contain it safely for this length of time. When humans come into contact with too much radiation they can be killed, get cancer and have genetically mutated children as seen in the Chernobyl nuclear power station disaster of 1986.

A dozen serious floods a year could become the norm in Britain as a result of global warming, an expert with the Environment Agency said yesterday.

His warning was given as insurers urged the government to set up a national disaster agency to deal with the threat to lives and property from hazards such as floods and storms.

Professor Brian Lee of Portsmouth University said: 'We in Britain are almost unique in the world in not having a government body charged with dealing with the issue.' Global warming forecasts meant that there would be more rain, higher wind speeds and other weather-related impacts on Britain as the century progressed.

The Times, 14 December 2000.

THE PROBLEMS OF NATURAL RESOURCES

Natural resources are naturally occurring materials such as oil and fertile land which can be used by humans. They can be divided into two types:

Renewable resources are resources which humans can use over and over again because they renew themselves. For example, wind power, solar power, water power, fertile land producing food, sugar cane (which can provide energy for cars) and soft woods (which grow very quickly and can be used for paper, furniture etc.). Such renewable resources cause no problems for human use.

These pipelines are taking oil from the North Sea which can never be replaced.

The British-based environmental group, Global Witness, which campaigned against large-scale illegal logging in Cambodia, has been appointed as a government-sanctioned independent monitor of its forestry sector. Global Witness will assist the Government to curb forest crime by inspections of commercial logging, national parks and border crossings.

The Times, 3 December 1999.

Finite or non-renewable resources are resources which disappear once they are used. For example, oil, coal, iron, tin, copper, uranium, natural gas, hard woods. Finite resources have major problems for human use because as the resource is used it becomes scarcer and scarcer and so can be used less and less.

The problem is most obvious in the case of oil. It is usually thought that a decline in the availability of oil would have the most effect on people's use of cars, but it is not only petrol and diesel which come from oil. All plastics and road surfaces, most candles, polishes, and chemical foodstuffs come from oil. Clearly, if the oil begins to dry up, there will be major effects on people's lives. Similarly, all the metals used in everyday living from car panels and railway tracks to pans and kitchen appliances come from finite ores.

Many scientists feel that unless we stop using these resources as we are, they will soon run out. This would mean no cars, no televisions, hi-fi's etc. In other words the problem of resources could have as severe consequences as the problem of pollution.

There are many arguments regarding what to do about environmental problems.

1 Many people feel that governments must do something to reduce pollution at international level. In 1997 55 industrial nations agreed to the Kyoto Protocol under which they resolved to cut their greenhouse gas emissions by an average of 5.2 per cent a year. One problem was that the world's biggest greenhouse gas polluter, the USA, would not sign. So, a new international conference was held at The Hague in November 2000. Although this did not end in any agreement, the United States did change its position and work has already begun for a further conference.

NON-RELIGIOUS ARGUMENTS ABOUT THE ENVIRONMENT

Britain is on course for a 23 per cent cutback in gases linked with global warming, the Government predicted yesterday, putting us at the head of the worldwide effort to avert climate change. Michael Meacher, the Environment Minister, said that Britain's efforts, however, would amount to little unless other countries adopted similar strategies.

The Times, 18 November 2000.

Britain's first power station producing electricity from waste is an attempt to preserve resources.

2 Many scientists believe that science and technology will find a solution to the problems. There are now several alternative ways of making electricity which do not produce carbon dioxide or nuclear waste: wind power, sea power (using either the waves or the tides), hydro-electric power (using the water in a dam) and solar power (using the sun's heat) are just a few which are now producing electricity. Car manufacturers are looking at water, sugar cane and electric batteries as ways of powering cars. Some car firms claim that by 2004 there will be fuel-cell cars on the market powered by the hydrogen from water. In the same way recycling will enable the lifetime of many resources to be extended. Some cars are now made of almost 75 per cent recycled materials.

It is also possible to improve the efficiency and reduce the pollution caused by such things as cars. It would take 50 small cars being produced in 1999 to produce the same amount of pollution that one small car made in 1976. By 2010 the total tonnage of pollutants emitted by cars will reduce by 75 per cent compared with 1992, even though the number of cars on the road will increase. Scientists are working on using chemicals from plants rather than oil to produce such things as plastics.

3 Some people think an alternative lifestyle is necessary and they only use natural products (e.g. clothes made from cotton or wool), eat organic foods (foods grown without fertilisers or pesticides) and ride bikes instead of owning a car. They believe that if everyone lived in this way, environmental problems would disappear.

In 1986 Christian, Muslim, Jewish, Sikh, Hindu and Buddhist leaders met in Assisi to mark the 25th anniversary of the World Wide Fund for Nature and made the Assisi Declaration promising their support for the conservation of the planet.

There are now many wind farms, like this one in Cornwall, producing pollution free, renewable electricity.

Christians believe that God created the universe and everything in the universe.

The Bible says that when God created the universe, he saw what he had made, and saw that it was good. This means that Christians have to regard the whole of creation as a gift from God, to be used by humans in the way in which God intended.

It is a basic belief of Christianity that God gave humans the stewardship of the earth and its resources. Stewardship means looking after something so that it can be passed on to the next generation. In the Parable of the Talents or Minas (Luke 19:11–26), Jesus taught that God expects humans to pass on to the next generation more than they have been given. Many Christians believe that this means Christians have a responsibility to leave the earth a better place than they found it.

The universe as a whole is a product of God's creative and imaginative will. All its parts are interdependent. Men and women are to be stewards and creators, not exploiters, of its resources, material, animal and spiritual. Christians must support those working for conservation and the development of more appropriate sustainable life-styles.

Christian Faith Concerning the Environment – Methodist Conference 1991.

God blessed them and said to them, 'Be fruitful and increase in number. Rule over the fish of the sea and the birds of the air and over every living creature that moves on the ground.'

Genesis 1:28

When I consider your heavens, the work of your fingers ... what is man that you are mindful of him? You made him a little lower than the heavenly beings ... You made him rule over the work of your hands; you put everything under his feet.

Psalm 8:3–6

Would Christian teachings make industry more environmentally friendly?

Motion at the General Synod of the Church of England 1992.

To leave the earth a better place than they found it means that such Christians not only try to reduce pollution and preserve resources, they also try to improve the quality of life of the less fortunate. Christian stewardship, for them, means a fair sharing of the earth's resources for everyone because of the teachings of Jesus in the Sermon on the Mount about sharing. So Christian stewardship can involve sharing the earth's resources more fairly and improving the standard of living in less-developed countries (LDCs) without causing more pollution.

All these teachings mean that Christians have a duty to share in and support the work of groups which try to reduce pollution and conserve resources. They also mean that individual Christians should be judging what they are doing in their lives by the standards of Christian stewardship. However, Christians believe humans have been placed in control of the earth by God and so in tackling environmental issues, human concerns cannot be ignored – for example shutting down a factory which causes pollution but employs three thousand people would not be a Christian solution.

Catechism of the Catholic Church.

Solar-powered houses help to preserve resources.

Islam teaches that the universe and everything in it was created by one God and so there is a unity in all of creation. One of the most important Muslim beliefs is called Tawhid. This means that there is only one God and nothing is to be in any way connected with God, but it also means that there is a unity in creation. This unity between humans can be seen in the Muslim Ummah and in the way in which the universe runs on scientific laws which are a unity.

Many Muslims believe there is a balance in the universe which is revealed in Tawhid and in Surah 55. This belief in the balance of the universe is like extending the idea of an ecosystem to the whole universe.

Muslims also believe that God created Adam as his Khalifah (vice-regent or vice-gerent – someone who looks after things for you). This means that all Muslims are God's khalifahs who have to keep the balance of creation and look after the earth for God by following the way of life set out for Muslims in the Qur'an and the Shari'ah.

Muslims believe that this life is a test from God on which they will be judged at the end of the world. A major part of the test is looking after the environment in the way of Islam.

On the Day of Judgement, Muslims believe that they will be questioned by God on the way they have looked after the earth and the life on earth. Those who have polluted or misused God's gifts will not be allowed into heaven.

These teachings and beliefs of Islam mean that Muslims must be involved in removing pollution and be involved in the preservation of the earth's resources. However, Muslims believe that humans have been placed in charge of the earth's resources by God and so in tackling environmental issues, the effects on humans cannot be ignored.

ISLAM AND THE ENVIRONMENT

> Behold thy Lord said to the angels, 'I will create a vice-gerent on earth.' ... And He taught Adam the nature of all things ... And behold, He said to the angels: 'Bow down to Adam.' And they bowed down: Not so Iblis: he refused and was haughty: He was of those who reject the faith.

Surah 2:30–34

> The sun and the moon follow courses exactly computed; And the herbs and the trees – both alike bow in adoration. And the firmament has He raised high, and He has set up the balance in order that ye may not transgress balance.

Surah 55:5–8

> The planet that we live on has been created by Allah and entrusted to mankind until the Day of Judgement. As His 'agents' on earth, we have the responsibility of looking after all of the other creatures, the plants, the atmosphere and everything else which surrounds us. It is important, therefore, for Muslims to play a leading part in the efforts to protect our environment. Life on earth is set up with natural balance and this is the key to our survival here.

What does Islam Say? Ibrahim Hewitt.

> Behold in the creation of the heavens and the earth; in the alternation of the night and the day ... in the rain which God sends down from the skies, and the life which He gives therewith ... in the beasts of all kinds that He scatters through the earth; in the change of the wind and the clouds ... here indeed are signs for a people that are wise.

Surah 2:164

JUDAISM AND THE ENVIRONMENT

Judaism also teaches that the earth belongs to God and humans have been given the task of looking after the world for God. Jews believe that the way God gave humans control of the life of the planet in Genesis chapter 1 means that God wanted people to use the earth's resources wisely without either waste or misuse.

In building towns and cities, Jews have to follow a principle set down in Numbers 35:2 known as the migrash. This states that around every town there must be an area of open land. This land cannot be used in any way, not even for growing crops. So every town should have a pleasant environment with a surrounding parkland available for everyone to use for recreation. The Talmud suggests that the migrash should be surrounded by a ring of fruit trees.

The Tees Barrage is helping to reduce pollution and prevent floods.

> God blessed them (male and female) and said to them, 'Be fruitful and increase in number; fill the earth and subdue it. Rule over the fish ... and the birds ... and over every living creature.'

Genesis 1:28

Another important Jewish principle connected with the environment is that of never destroying anything needlessly. In biblical times when an army was attacking a town, it would lay siege to it by building a wooden wall so that no one could get out. Deuteronomy 20 says that Jewish armies are not allowed to cut down fruit trees for these walls. Later rabbis took this to mean that Jews must never destroy things of the earth which are useful. Rabbi Joseph Schneerson told a story of how, when he was a boy and plucked a leaf off a tree, his father told him, 'Everything in nature is put there to serve God's purpose. We can use them for our needs, but we must be careful not to destroy things unnecessarily.'

> **When you lay siege to a city for a long time ... do not destroy its trees by putting an axe to them ... Do not cut them down. Are the trees of the fields people, that you should besiege them?**
>
> *Deuteronomy 20:19*

> **Command the Israelites to give the Levites towns ... And give them pasture-lands around the towns ... The pasture-lands around the towns will extend fifteen hundred feet from the town wall.**
>
> *Numbers 35:2*

The respect for the land and for trees is shown in the special Jewish festival of Tu B'Shevat (New Year for Trees). This marks the new agricultural year in Israel at the end of January or the beginning of February. The New Year for Trees is celebrated by planting trees in areas where they are needed or by paying someone to plant one in such a country. It is also shown in the practice of Jubilee years. Leviticus 25 orders Jews that every 50 years they must not plant crops or harvest such things as fruit trees, nature must have a chance to recharge its batteries.

All these teachings and beliefs mean that Jews must be concerned about environmental issues and support the work of groups which are trying to stop pollution, end waste and use resources responsibly. However, like Christians and Muslims, they believe that human interests come first and that environmental issues cannot ignore the human issues.

> People are beginning to regard themselves as just another part of the ecosystem. In Jewish thinking, such a view is misguided and dangerous. It leads to denying the supreme value of human beings... For Jews, environmental concerns have to take into account the special place of humanity in creation. In other words, they have to have a moral dimension.
>
> *Moral Issues in Judaism*, Arye Forta.

> **The earth is the Lord's, and everything in it, the world and all who live in it.**
>
> *Psalm 24:1*

HINDUISM AND THE ENVIRONMENT

Hindus believe that there is a oneness in the universe and in nature which was created by God, and in which God is present. Most Hindus believe that there is an eternal law of nature and that the human soul should seek some form of union with this nature to find God and peace. This means that humans should not exploit or abuse nature, they should work with nature. Hindus have to work with the earth to produce crops and Hinduism teaches farmers that if they respect the earth, it will give them its treasures. The Hindu belief that God is a part of the earth he has created is a major reason for Hindus to respect the earth.

Hinduism also respects animal life. In his avatars, Vishnu appeared as a fish, a tortoise, a boar and a lion. Krishna was a cowherd. Many Hindus believe that they may have been animals in previous incarnations. So animals are respected and many Hindus believe that the teachings on ahimsa (non-violence) mean that they should be vegetarians refusing to take any form of life because they have respect for all life. Almost all Hindus regard the cow as sacred because of its connections with Krishna.

The waters are the body of breath, and the moon up there is its luminous appearance. So, the extent of the waters and of that moon is the same as the extent of breath. Now, all of these are of equal extent, all are without limit. So those who venerate them as finite win only a limited world, whereas those who venerate them as infinite win a world without limit.

Upanishad 1:5:13

Peace of sky, peace of mid-region,

peace of earth, peace of waters, peace of plants.

Peace of trees, peace of all gods, peace of Brahman,

peace of the universe, peace of peace,

May that peace come to me.

Yajur-veda VS 36.17

The Hindu custom of planting trees helps to make the soil more fertile.

Forests are very special to Hindus. The third ashrama after the householder is the forest dweller (vanaprastha). The forests are pure nature untouched by humans and it is in living here that Hindus can find union with God. According to Hindu stories, Krishna spent much of his time in the forest which also makes them very special places. Certain trees are thought to be especially holy, for example the banyan tree is thought to be holy because it was whilst sitting under a banyan tree that the Buddha became enlightened.

This is perhaps why the major Hindu green group, the Chipko, began with tree hugging. About 300 years ago, the followers of a Hindu sect led by a woman, Amitra Devi, decided to protect trees from the woodcutters by embracing the trees so that the woodcutters would harm them rather than the trees. In 1974 a group of village women in Garhwal hugged the trees which were about to be chopped down for a sports goods company as they knew it would ruin their lives. Some Hindu thinkers then remembered Jambeshwar who, in the fifteenth century, had a dream that human beings would be destroyed because they had destroyed nature. So the Chipko (hug-the-tree) movement began, mainly with women, determined that India's rapid industrialisation should not destroy the environment.

These teachings and beliefs mean that many Hindus have a great respect for the environment. Nevertheless, some Hindus feel that as humans are the most advanced life-form, they have been given the right to use the earth's resources in any way they think is right. There is a lot of conflict in India today between those Hindus who want industrial progress regardless of the environment and those who think the environment must be protected from industry.

> **May men and oxen both plough in contentment, in contentment the plough cleave the furrow. Auspicious furrow, we venerate you. We pray you, bless us and bring us abundant harvests.**
>
> *Rig Veda IV.57*

> Indian civilisation has been distinctive in locating its source of regeneration, material and intellectual, in the forest, not in the city. India's best ideas have come where man was in communion with trees and rivers and lakes, away from the crowds. The peace of the forest has helped the intellectual development of man.
>
> Rabindranath Tagore in *Tapovana*.

RELIGIOUS GROUPS AND THE ENVIRONMENT

A Christian Aid project of planting seedlings and fruit bushes to prevent soil erosion.

All religions have groups which are working to steward and conserve the environment. In Christianity, groups like Christian Aid try to ensure that their work in world development also protects the environment. For example in Columbia, South America, Christian Aid is involved in preventing deforestation by developers and encouraging the native farmers to develop environmentally friendly alternative farming methods. There are also Christian groups which are specifically concerned with the environment. For example, Target Earth is a British Christian group active in 15 countries buying up endangered lands, saving the jaguar, reforesting ravaged terrain. Similarly Muslim Aid is working to conserve the environment in Afghanistan and there are Muslim environmental groups such as The Islamic Foundation for Ecology and Environmental Sciences. Hindu environmental groups are outlined in Factfile 13. There are several Jewish environmental groups such as Hadassah and the B'nai B'rith Youth Organization.

Target Earth is providing a unique and critical opportunity for a new generation of Christians who care about God's earth. As the Church enters the new millennium, Christians will be looking to this group to lead us forward. We are enthusiastic for this organization, personally involved with it and grateful to God for its work.

Tom Sine and Christine Aroney-Sine, Global development specialists.

In 1993 the Eden Conservancy was established to counter the problems of deforestation and the ensuing human suffering. The idea was simple and visionary – to buy up the world's endangered lands. There seemed no better way to protect God's good creation. Working with local conservation groups, specific locations were selected for preservation. One such property is 8,000 acres of rainforest in Belize, Central America, that will help expand the Blue Hole National Park – a region where jaguar, toucans and mahogany trees flourish. When protected with the help of the Belize Audubon Society (the American equivalent of the RSPB), this area will serve as a reminder of the majesty and beauty of God's handiwork.

From a Target Earth pamphlet.

The work of the Jewish National Fund (JNF)

Although not all Jews agree with the establishment of Israel, Jews from all over the world do regard Israel as a holy land and so they want to remove pollution and make sure resources are being used properly and carefully. The Jewish National Fund takes donations from Jews all over the world and uses them to improve the environment in Israel. It is a religious organisation following the mitzvot of Judaism.

1 A major work of the JNF is to educate Jews outside Israel about the work of the Fund and collect donations from them to use in Israel.

2 The JNF has planted 200 million trees. These trees not only reduce the greenhouse effect and provide outdoor recreation, they are actively used by the JNF to halt desertification. Much of Israel is next to desert land and the trees prevent the soil erosion which allows deserts to spread. Timna Park near Eilat on the Red Sea is a woodland park which JNF created out of the desert. However, forests can cause major ecological problems if a fire breaks out and so the JNF has developed techniques for preventing and controlling forest fires in hot climates.

3 The JNF has a very successful programme of rolling back the desert. It developed the technique known as 'savannisation'. This is based on planting things much further apart than normal and watering them by capturing the small amounts of rain and surface runoff in special holes. This has led to quite large areas of the northern Negev Desert (where annual rainfall is only 10–26 cm) becoming available for agriculture.

4 The JNF backs up its savannisation by building reservoirs and dams to capture the floodwaters of the desert areas. These can then be used to replenish underground aquifers, breed fish, halt soil erosion and irrigate fields for agriculture.

5 JNF also deals with health hazards such as waste dumps, landfills and abandoned quarries. It makes them safe by using proven environmentally friendly methods and has created a unique landscape of groundwater pools in Nitzanim Park in the desert out of a dangerous abandoned quarry.

In all its work, the Jewish National Fund believes that it is putting into practice the teachings of Judaism on care for the environment.

Rolling back the desert in the northern sections of the Negev.

ANIMAL RIGHTS ISSUES

Animal rights means the belief that animals have rights not to be exploited by humans. There are several issues connected with this:

Can animals have rights?

Some thinkers argue that animals cannot have rights because to have rights requires being self-conscious and autonomous. Self-conscious means being able to see oneself as a separate entity with a past and a future. Autonomous means being able to choose how to live one's life. Animals do not appear to be self-conscious and certainly are not able to choose how to live their lives because animals have to adapt themselves to fit their environment, whereas humans adapt their environment to fit their needs (e.g. if the weather gets colder, only those animals with the most fur will survive whereas humans just turn up the central heating).

Other thinkers argue that young children are not self-conscious or autonomous and yet we believe they have rights. Also there is now evidence from work with apes, chimpanzees and gorillas that some animals are self-conscious.

Other thinkers argue that there can only be rights for those who are capable of protecting their rights and no animal is capable of that – they have to rely on humans.

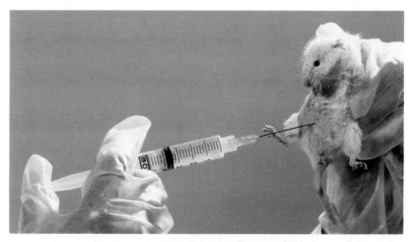

A scientist searching for a cure for Aids injects a mouse.

Should animals be used in experiments?

There are many arguments on this which can be summarised as:

For experimenting on animals	Against experimenting on animals
• Animals do not have the same rights as humans	• Animals have the same rights not to be abused as humans.
• Human health is more important than animal welfare	• Ignoring animal welfare degrades humans and makes the people who experiment on animals sub-human
• Most advances in human health have come from research on animals	• Better hygiene and nutrition have had more effect in improving human health than animal experiments
• The public expects high standards of drug safety and these can only be achieved by experiments on animals	• There are alternatives to the use of animals and if these cannot be used, then the drugs should not be used

Should animals be used for food?

Arguments for eating animals	Arguments against eating animals
• Humans are omnivores with meat-eating teeth so nature intends them to eat meat	• Humans do not need to eat meat to live
• Other animals eat meat	• Some animals are herbivores
• Killing animals for food is different from killing for fun and is done humanely	• Killing animals always causes suffering
• If animals were not eaten there would be much more cruelty to animals because what would happen to the millions of animals farmers would set free to fend for themselves	• Ending meat eating would not happen suddenly and ways would have to be thought of for dealing with the animals. In the end, nature would achieve a balance

More and more people believe we should only eat eggs from hens that live a normal life (free range).

There are:

44 million sheep
12 million cattle
8 million pigs
128 million hens, ducks, geese
kept on farms in Britain

Source: Meat and Livestock Commission.

Research on animals has discovered many medical treatments including: the use of insulin for diabetes, antibiotics, treatments for leukaemia, the use of ventolin for asthma.

Source: The Biomedical Research Trust.

Vivisection literally means the cutting up of living creatures. It is now widely used to describe all the painful experiments performed, throughout the world, on between 100 and 200 million living animals every year. In Britain alone over 13 000 researchers working in more than 300 licensed establishments annually carry out experiments on well over 2.5 million animals. Animals received no anaesthetic in 63 per cent of these experiments.

Source: British Union for the Abolition of Vivisection (BUAV).

CHRISTIANITY AND ANIMAL RIGHTS

> Then God said, 'Let us make man in our image, in our likeness, and let them rule over the fish of the sea and the birds of the air, over the livestock, over all the earth, and over all the creatures that move along the ground.'

Genesis 1:26

> Are not two sparrows sold for a penny? Yet not one of them will fall to the ground apart from the will of your father.

Matthew 10:29

The Christian tradition asserts that animals have been created by God and that they have an intrinsic value for that reason. Nevertheless, the value of animals has always been seen as secondary to that of human beings made in God's image and placed in a central position in creation. Human beings have both an affinity with and an obligation to animals.

Our Responsibility for the Living Environment report by the Church of England Board for Social Responsibility.

Let the law of kindness know no limits. Show a loving consideration for all God's creatures.

General Advice to Quakers 1928

All Christians agree that animals are part of God's creation and that humans have duties towards animals.

Most Christians believe that humans should not be cruel to animals:

- farmers should care for their livestock humanely;
- animals for food should be slaughtered without pain;
- animals should only be used for scientific experiments when it is absolutely necessary.

However, they believe that humans have a right to use animals for food and for experiments which are aimed at improving human health or testing new drugs, toiletries and foods for health and safety.

They believe this because:

- God is the creator of animals as well as humans;
- God gave humans the right to control animals;
- animals do not have rights since only humans can have rights because they are the only beings made in the image of God;
- humans have a duty to care for animals because of their duty as stewards of God's creation.

Some Christians are vegetarians and are opposed to animals being used either for food or for experiments. They also oppose the hunting of animals and fishing. They believe this because:

- God is the creator of animals as well as humans;
- humans have a duty to care for animals as part of their duty as stewards of God's creation;
- Christians should never be cruel as Jesus said he was the good shepherd who would lay down his life for his sheep rather than let them be harmed;
- it is impossible to slaughter animals for food or experiment on them without being cruel;
- animals have the same rights as humans.

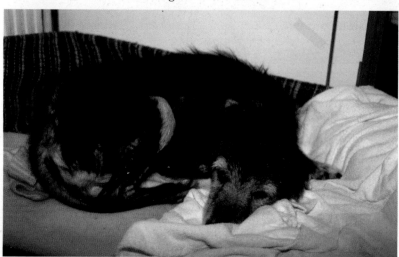

There is a Christian tradition of preventing cruelty to animals.

Muslims believe that humans should not be cruel to animals:

- farmers should care for their livestock humanely;
- animals for food should be slaughtered without pain;
- animals should only be used for scientific experiments when it is absolutely necessary;
- hunting can only be done for food, not sport

However, they believe that humans have a right to use animals for food and for experiments which are aimed at improving human health or testing new drugs, toiletries and foods for health and safety.

They believe this because:

- the Qur'an says that animals are part of God's creation;
- the Qur'an teaches that animals have feelings and must be dedicated to God when slaughtered in a painless way;
- the Qur'an states that humans may use certain animals for food;
- there are many hadith about treating animals kindly;
- the Shari'ah teaches that animals can be used for experiments but only if they are necessary and for the benefit of humans.

ISLAM AND ANIMAL RIGHTS

> **There is not an animal that lives on the earth, nor a being that flies on its wings, but forms part of communities like you. Nothing have we omitted from the Book and they all shall be gathered to their Lord in the end.**
>
> *Surah 6:38*

> **Seest thou not that it is God whose praises all beings in the heavens and on earth do celebrate, and the birds of the air with wings outspread? Each one knows its own mode of prayer and praise. And God knows well all that they do.**
>
> *Surah 24:41*

His trustees are responsible for maintaining the unity of his creation, the integrity of the earth, its flora and fauna, its wildlife and natural environment.

Muslim Declaration from Assisi 1986

The following acts are abominable regarding the slaughtering of animals: to slaughter an animal at a place where another animal can see it; to slaughter an animal which someone has bred and brought up himself.

Articles of Islamic Acts, the Al-Khoei Foundation.

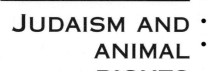
JUDAISM AND ANIMAL RIGHTS

Most Jews believe that humans should not be cruel to animals:

- farmers should care for their livestock humanely;
- animals for food should be slaughtered without pain;
- animals should only be used for scientific experiments when it is absolutely necessary.

However, they believe that humans have a right to use animals for food and for experiments which are aimed at improving human health or testing new drugs, toiletries and foods for health and safety.

> Then God said, 'Let us make man in our image, in our likeness, and let them rule over the fish of the sea and the birds of the air, over the livestock, over all the earth, and over all the creatures that move along the ground.'

Genesis 1:26

They believe this because:

- God created animals and so they must be given respect;
- animal life cannot have the same value as human life because animals are not made in God's image;
- God gave humans control over animals;
- the Torah allows animals to be used for human benefit, but does not allow any form of animal cruelty;
- the Talmud lays down strict laws on humane treatment of animals including that a farmer must not buy more animals than he can afford to feed.

> A righteous man cares for the needs of his animal.

Proverbs 12:10

Some Jews are vegetarians because they feel that it is impossible to be a meat eater without being cruel to animals and cruelty to animals is banned by the Torah.

Teachers must see that children respect the smallest and largest animals which, like people, have feelings. The child who gets enjoyment from the convulsions of an injured beetle will grow up to be insensitive to human suffering.

Statement by Rabbi Samson Raphael Hirsch.

> The fear and dread of you will fall upon all the beasts of the earth and all the birds of the air, upon every creature that moves along the ground, and upon all the fish of the sea, they are given into your hands. Everything that lives and moves will be food for you.

Genesis 9:2–3

Kosher shops ensure that food has been prepared properly and humanely.

Cows are allowed to roam freely in India.

Hindus will not kill cows and so do not eat beef. Cows are regarded as sacred and can never be harmed. In many Indian states the killing of cows is banned and there are special retirement homes for animals (mainly cows) called gowshalas. Indian businessmen in the UK even offered to take the cows that were slaughtered because of BSE to retirement in India. Hindus regard the cow as sacred because:

- the bull is the animal on which Shiva rides;

- when Krishna came to earth, he worked as a cowherd and dairyman and so made cows sacred;

- cows provide so much for life – milk, butter and yoghurt, bullock transport and plough-pulling, dung for manure, fuel and building materials.

Hindus believe that animals have rights to protection from harm and cruelty. They do not approve of experiments on animals. Most Hindus are vegetarians, they will not kill any animals. They believe this because:

- Hindus believe that the atman is in all living things, so that God is in them and so harming animals is like harming God;

- the belief in ahimsa means that violence is wrong if used against animals;

- the Law of Manu says that any form of slaughtering is a sin;

- in the Gita, Krishna only eats fruit and vegetables;

- the belief in rebirth and karma means that people who slaughter animals will themselves be slaughtered in their next lives;

- animals are closely connected with the gods – Ganesha is an elephant, Hanuman a monkey, Vishnu has appeared as a fish, a tortoise and a boar.

I went from Bengala into the country of Couche. Here they all be gentiles and will kill nothing. They have hospitals for sheepe, goates, dogs, cats, birds, and for all other living creatures. When they be olde and lame, they keep them till they die.

From the records of the travels of Ralph Fetch who visited India in the sixteenth century (quoted from *Hinduism,* K M Sen).

A householder should regard deer, camels, donkeys, mice, snakes, birds and bees as his sons: for what difference is there between his sons and them?

Bhagavata Purana 7, 14, 9

Sweet be our Father heaven to us.

For us may the forest tree be full of sweetness,

full of sweetness the sun,

and full of sweetness the cows for us.

Rig Veda I.90:6–8

He who offers to me with devotion only a leaf, or a flower, or a fruit, or even a little water, this I accept from that yearning soul because with a pure heart it was offered with love. Whatever you do, or eat, or give, or offer in adoration, let it be an offering to me.

Bhagavad Gita 9:26–27

Where do you seek your God, overlooking him in various forms in front of you? He serves God best, who is kind to all living creatures.

Swami Vivekananda (quoted from *Themes and Issues in Hinduism,* P Bowen).

QUESTIONS

Factfiles 7 The dangers of pollution, 8 The problems of natural resources and 9 Non-religious arguments about the environment

1 What is an ecosystem?

2 Make a list of things humans are doing which will damage the earth's ecosystem.

3 Explain why resources are likely to be a problem in the future.

4 Make a list of the things people are doing to reduce the problem of resources.

5 Make a list of things people are doing to reduce the problem of pollution.

6 Have a class discussion on the topic, 'People worry too much about the environment.'

Factfile 10 Christianity and the environment

1 What is meant by Christian stewardship?

2 On what biblical teachings is stewardship based?

3 Explain how a parable Jesus told helps Christians in their attitude to the environment.

Factfiles 11, 12, 13 Islam, Judaism and Hinduism and the environment

1 Choose one religion other than Christianity and write down what it teaches about the correct use of the environment.

2 Give three reasons for these teachings.

3 'If people took their religion seriously, there would be no environmental problems.'
Do you agree? Give reasons for your opinion, showing that you have considered another point of view. In your answer, you should refer to at least one religion.

Factfile 14 Religious groups and the environment

Explain how one religious agency is trying to improve the environment.

Factfile 15 Animal rights issues

1 State three arguments in favour of research on animals.

2 Give three arguments against research on animals.

3 Explain why some people are vegetarians.

Factfile 16 Christianity and animal rights

1 Give an outline of Christian teachings on animal rights.

2 Explain why some Christians are opposed to medical research being carried out on animals.

3 Have a class discussion on whether Christians should be vegetarians.

Factfiles 17, 18, 19 Islam, Judaism and Hinduism and animal rights

1 Choose one religion other than Christianity and give an outline of its teachings on animal rights.

2 'Religion does not help animal rights.'
Do you agree? Give reasons for your opinion, showing that you have considered another point of view. In your answer, you should refer to at least one religion.

❸ RELIGION: PEACE AND CONFLICT

NUCLEAR WEAPONS – WEAPONS BASED ON ATOMIC FISSION OR FUSION.

OTHER WEAPONS OF MASS DESTRUCTION – NON-NUCLEAR WEAPONS WHICH CAN DESTROY LARGE AREAS AND/OR LARGE NUMBERS OF PEOPLE E.G. CHEMICAL WEAPONS.

PACIFISM – REFUSING TO FIGHT IN WARS.

JUST WAR – A WAR THAT IS FOUGHT FOR THE RIGHT REASONS AND IN A RIGHT WAY.

WORLD PEACE – THE BASIC AIM OF THE UNITED NATIONS TO REMOVE THE CAUSES OF WAR.

BULLYING – INTIMIDATING OR FRIGHTENING PEOPLE WEAKER THAN YOURSELF.

FORGIVENESS – THE ACT OF STOPPING BLAMING SOMEONE AND/OR PARDONING THEM FOR WHAT THEY HAVE DONE WRONG.

RECONCILIATION – BRINGING TOGETHER PEOPLE WHO WERE OPPOSED TO EACH OTHER.

Most people approve of peace and disapprove of war. In 1945, the United Nations was established with the aim of keeping world peace and making sure that there was never another world war.

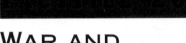

WAR AND PEACE ISSUES

The United Nations Headquarters in New York is on independent territory given to the UN by the United States government.

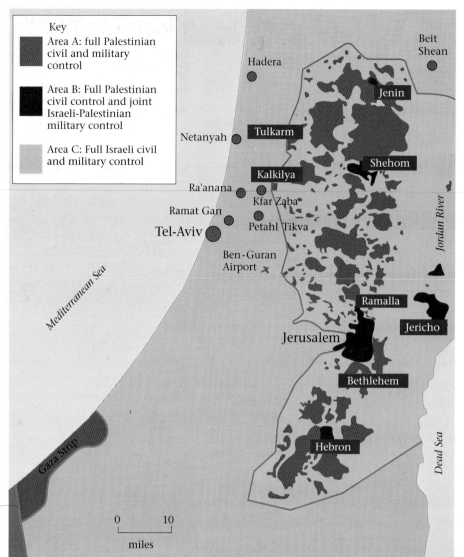

Key

Area A: full Palestinian civil and military control

Area B: Full Palestinian civil control and joint Israeli-Palestinian military control

Area C: Full Israeli civil and military control

Beit Shean

Hadera

Jenin

Tulkarm

Netanyah

Shehom

Kalkilya

Ra'anana

Kfar Zaba

Ramat Gan

Petahl Tikva

Tel-Aviv

Ben-Guran Airport

Mediterranean Sea

Jordan River

Ramalla

Jericho

Jerusalem

Bethlehem

Dead Sea

Hebron

Gaza Strip

0   10
miles

Israel and Palestine after the Oslo agreement.

The Holy Mount in Jerusalem causes trouble because it is claimed by Jews, Christians and Muslims.

However, since 1945 there have been many wars which have threatened to become world wars, and in which both sides claimed to be justified. The main examples from the past were the Korean War (1950–53) fought between the United Nations defending South Korea and China supporting North Korea; and the Vietnam War (1961–75) fought between North Vietnam supported by the USSR and China, and South Vietnam supported by the USA and Australia.

There are many areas of conflict in the world today, the specification requires you to know of one in detail and one briefly.

1 Israel and Palestine

There is conflict in the Middle East between the State of Israel and the Palestinian people who want the restoration of a Palestinian State. A potential Palestinian State was established after the Oslo Agreement (1993–95), but Israel still has its army in Palestinian areas and there is no agreement as to Palestinian independence and borders. An important point of disagreement is the city of Jerusalem which both Israelis and Palestinians claim as their capital and which is a holy city for Jews, Muslims and Christians.

The main reasons for the conflict are:

• The State of Israel existed as a Jewish state from about 1000 BCE to 132 CE when the Romans banned Jews from living in Palestine after they revolted against Roman rule.

• After the Arabs captured the area from the Romans (the Byzantine Empire) in 636 CE, Palestine became an Arab state as part of the Arab Empire.

• During the First World War, Britain captured Palestine from the Ottoman Empire and promised an independent state to the Palestinians and a national homeland to the Jews.

- After the First World War, Britain ruled Palestine on behalf of the League of Nations and many Jews emigrated from Europe to set up their national homeland and to escape from fascism (right-wing, anti-Jewish political parties such as Hitler's Nazis).

- After the Second World War, the Jews revolted against British rule and set up the State of Israel.

- This state was recognised by the United Nations in 1948 and those parts of Palestine not in the new State of Israel became part of the State of Jordan.

- In a war fought between Israel and the neighbouring Arab states in 1967, Israel occupied all those parts of the State of Jordan west of the River Jordan to protect her borders (these areas are known as the West Bank and are the basis for the new state of Palestine).

- Israel was ordered to give up the occupied territories by the United Nations, but has refused to do so until the Palestinians and the neighbouring Arab states recognise Israel's borders.

2 Kashmir

Kashmir is a large area between the North of India and the East of Pakistan. South Kashmir is a province of India. The majority of the population of Kashmir is Muslim and several Muslim groups are fighting to make Kashmir a part of Pakistan (which is a Muslim state) rather than being a part of India which is mainly Hindu (though there are many Hindus in Kashmir and there are actually more Muslims in India than in Pakistan). The Indian and Pakistanis armies have forces on the border and fighting has never really stopped since 1949.

The main reasons for this conflict are:

- when India gained independence from Britain in 1947, the majority Muslim areas in the North West and North East were made into the State of Pakistan (the eastern part became independent from Pakistan in 1971 and is now Bangladesh);

- Kashmir was ruled by a Hindu maharajah in 1947 and he decided to join India;

- the large numbers of Hindus, who form a substantial minority of the population, do not want to join Pakistan;

- the Indian government regards Kashmir as an important buffer between India and Pakistan and India and China and will not give up the area.

A major problem in world conflict and world peace is that so many countries have weapons of mass destruction including chemical and nuclear weapons. A war fought with such weapons could destroy the world which is why President Bush is proposing to develop a missile defence system which would destroy any nuclear weapons attacking the USA before they could reach US airspace.

India, Pakistan and Israel all have nuclear weapons.

Powell insists defence rests on 'Star Wars'

Immediately after he was nominated to be Secretary of State by President-elect Bush, General Powell told reporters that a national missile defence system was necessary to prevent the blackmail inherent in Third World regimes possessing nuclear weapons with which they think they could hold the US hostage.

Adapted from a *Times* report, 18 December 2000.

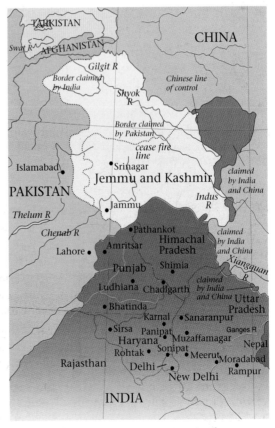

CHRISTIANITY AND WAR

> **Blessed are the peacemakers, for they will be called sons of God.**

Matthew 5:9

> **I tell you, do not resist an evil person. If someone strikes you on the right cheek, turn to him the other also.**

Matthew 5:39

> **You have heard that it was said, 'Love your neighbour and hate your enemy.' But I tell you: Love your enemies and pray for those who persecute you.**

Matthew 5:43–44

> How can Christians wage war, or even become soldiers in peace-time without the sword which our Lord has taken away.

Tertullian, a second-century Christian thinker.

> We utterly deny all outward wars and strife and fighting with outward weapons, for any end, or under any pretence whatever, this is our testimony to the whole world.

A Declaration from the Harmless and Innocent People of God called Quakers presented to King Charles II.

All Christians believe that they are called to bring peace to the world. The message of the angels when Jesus was born was 'On earth peace to men' (Luke 2:14). Jesus said that those working for peace will be called sons of God. The New Testament is full of references to peace and the way in which Christians should be bringing peace and reconciliation. The Christian Churches all make regular statements opposing war and encouraging their members to work for peace. However, they also realise that it is not always possible to avoid war. So although all Christians are against war and must work for peace, there are two different Christian attitudes to how Christians should behave if a war occurs.

1 Christian Pacifism

Pacifism means refusing to fight in wars and, for the first 300 years of Christianity, Christians refused to fight in wars. The great Christian leaders (e.g. Origen, Tertullian and Cyprian) all argued that Christians must not be involved in war and must be pacifists. However, when the Roman Empire became Christian things changed so that by 438, the Emperor Theodosius could issue a law that only Christians could fight in the Roman Army.

This memorial for those who suffered for the right to refuse to fight in wars (conscientious objectors) is in the Peace Garden, Tavistock Square, London.

In the twentieth century many Christians have become pacifists. They feel that the way modern warfare affects so many innocent people means that war can never be justified. There are many Christian pacifist groups, the largest being the Catholic group Pax Christi. The Quakers, Plymouth Brethren and Christadelphians are completely pacifist Churches. Some Christian pacifists refuse to be involved in any kind of violence and would not resist anyone who attacked them.

The reasons for Christian pacifism are:

- the teachings of Jesus about turning the other cheek and loving your enemies;
- the belief that peace will only come if people refuse to fight in wars;
- the horrible things that have happened to civilians in wars (especially the effects of the Hiroshima and Nagasaki nuclear bombs);
- the fifth commandment bans killing;
- Jesus stopped Peter from using violence when the soldiers came to arrest him with the words, 'Put your sword back in its place for all who draw the sword will die by the sword.'

2 Christians and the Just War

St Augustine first put forward reasons which would justify Christians in fighting in a war. These were developed by St Thomas Aquinas into what is now known as the Just War. Most Churches agree that Christians are justified in fighting in a war if:

- the cause of the war is just (resisting aggression or removing a great injustice);

- the war is being fought by the authority of a government or the United Nations;

- it is being fought with the intention of restoring peace;

- it is begun as a last resort (all non-violent methods of ending the dispute have been tried and failed);

- there is a reasonable chance of success (lives should not be wasted if there is no chance of achieving the aims which justify the deaths);

- the methods used avoid killing civilians (though this would not involve such things as bombs aimed at armaments factories hitting hospitals accidentally);

- the methods used must be proportional to the cause (it would not be possible to justify destroying a country with nuclear weapons because it had invaded a small island).

These rules would justify fighting in such wars as The Falklands War, The Gulf War and fighting for the United Nations in Bosnia, Kosovo etc.

> To the Christian serving in the armed forces of the 'Western democracies' there is the added assurance and comfort that their purpose is for defence and to maintain peace, not for selfish wars of aggression. The role of the Forces is almost entirely analogous to that of a police force … Therefore a Christian can regard it as an honour, and as a duty to be faithfully followed, should God call him to serve in these armed forces.

From *Christians and War* published by the Officers' Christian Union.

The reasons for the Christian just war theory are:

- St Paul said in Romans 13 and Titus 3 that Christians have to obey the orders of the government;

- Jesus never condemned the soldiers he met and actually commended the faith of the Roman Centurion in Luke 7;

- when Jesus was asked about paying taxes he said, 'Give to Caesar what is Caesar's' which must mean fighting in a just war ordered by the government;

- everyone agrees that a police force is needed to protect innocent people from criminals, in the same way an army ready to fight just wars is needed to protect innocent countries from criminal ones.

Austrian soldiers behind the Russian Front, 1916. The Austrian invasion of Serbia began the First World War.

> He (Jesus) said to them, 'But now if you have a purse, take it, and also a bag; and if you don't have a sword, sell your cloak and buy one.'

Luke 22:36

> Everyone must submit himself to the governing authorities, for there is no authority except that which God has established. The authorities that exist have been established by God.

Romans 13:1

> As long as the danger of war persists and there is no international authority with the necessary competence and power, governments cannot be denied the right of lawful self-defence, once all peace efforts have failed.

Catechism of the Catholic Church.

ISLAM AND WAR

Fight in the cause of God those who fight you, but do not transgress the limits; for God loveth not the transgressors.

Surah 2:190

Think not of those who are slain in God's way as dead. Nay, they live, finding their sustenance in the presence of the Lord.

Surah 3:169

Jaber reported that the Messenger of Allah said, 'War is a deception'.

Hadith quoted by Bukhari and Muslim.

Islam is not in favour of wars. One meaning of the word Islam is peace. The greeting used by all Muslims when they meet each other is 'salaam aleikum' – 'May peace be with you.' No true Muslim can possibly regard war as a good thing.

Ruqaiyyah Maqsood, *Teach Yourself Islam.*

Anas reported that the Messenger of Allah said, 'March in the name of Allah, and with the succour of Allah and over the religion of the Messenger of Allah! Kill not the emaciated old, nor the young children, nor the women'.

Hadith quoted by Abu Daud.

There is no idea of pacifism or turning the other cheek in Islam. The Qur'an encourages all Muslims to 'struggle in the way of Islam'.

The Arabic word for struggle is jihad which is often translated as holy war. However, Muslims believe in two forms of jihad, the greater and the lesser. The greater jihad is the struggle to make yourself and your society perfectly Muslim. This involves struggling with yourself and your desires, and not fighting. Lesser jihad is the struggle with forces outside yourself by means of war.

There are strict rules in Islam about when a war can be fought justifiably by Muslims:

- it must be fought for a just cause (either Islam is being attacked, or people are suffering an injustice, or in self-defence);
- it must be a last resort (all possible non-violent methods of solving the problem must have been tried);
- it must be authorised and led by a Muslim authority;
- it must be fought in such a way as to cause the minimum amount of suffering;
- innocent civilians (especially the old, the young, and women) must not be attacked;
- it must be ended as soon as the enemy lays down his arms.

All Muslims would agree that if a war fulfils these conditions then a Muslim must fight in it. The reasons for this view are:

- the Qur'an says that Muslims must fight if they are attacked and Muslims believe the Qur'an is the word of God;
- Muhammad is the great example for Muslims in how to live and he fought in wars;
- Muhammad made many statements (hadith) about war which say that Muslims must fight in just wars;
- the Qur'an says that anyone who dies fighting in a just war will go straight to heaven.

Muslims often protest against unjust wars.

Not all Jews approve of Israel's attitude to war.

JUDAISM AND WAR

Peace is the ideal for all Jews. Jews have always used 'Shalom alaykum' – 'peace be with you' instead of hello. The perfect society which Jews call the Messianic Age is thought of in terms of peace when 'they will beat their swords into ploughshares and their spears into pruning hooks. Nation will not take up sword against nation, nor will they train for war any more.' (Isaiah 2:4).

However, although Jews should seek peace, there is no concept of pacifism in Judaism. The Tenakh is full of accounts of wars in which God has been involved. So Judaism believes that it is acceptable to fight in wars under certain conditions. These are:

- if God has commanded it (as when God ordered Joshua to fight for the Promised Land);

- if they are attacked by an enemy;

- using a pre-emptive strike to stop an enemy from attacking when they are about to attack;

- going to the aid of a country that has been attacked;

- any other type of war can only be fought if there are good reasons for it, if all peaceful attempts have been tried and failed and if it is approved by the supreme council of Jewish rabbis.

The first four types of war are called *milchemet mitzvah* and must be fought. The last type is called *milchemet reshut* and is optional. Wars fought to gain revenge or to take things from other countries are banned.

The reasons for Jewish attitudes to war are:

- a mitzvah is a command from God which all Jews have to obey so they have to take part in a milchemet mitzvah;

- in the Tenakh there are many accounts of how Israel was able to keep her independence by defending herself when attacked;

- the experience of Jews before and during the Second World War was that without a Jewish army to defend them, six million Jews were murdered by the Nazis in the Holocaust.

Even so, all Jews work for and want peace.

> **If your enemy is hungry, give him food to eat; if he is thirsty, give him water to drink.**
>
> *Proverbs 25:21*

> **Turn from evil and do good; seek peace and pursue it.**
>
> *Psalm 34:14*

> The Torah was given to establish peace.
>
> *Midrash*

> The sword comes to the world because of delay of justice and through perversion of justice.
>
> *Talmud*

> **The law will go out from Zion, the word of the Lord from Jerusalem. He will judge between many peoples and will settle disputes for strong nations far and wide. They will beat their swords into ploughshares and their spears into pruning hooks. Nation will not take up sword against nation, nor will they train for war any more.**
>
> *Micah 4:3*

HINDUISM AND WAR

Hindus are dedicated to peace. At the end of all their prayers they pray for peace of mind and body, for peace from natural disaster and for peace from other people.

Hindus are very tolerant of other ideas and beliefs and many of the Hindu gurus of the past 100 years have been trying to show a peaceful way through the hatred and violence which religion can bring. However, not all Hindus are opposed to war and so there are two attitudes to war in Hinduism.

1 Pacifism and non-violence

Some Hindus believe that violence in any form is wrong and that Hindus should not take part in wars. India fought the only non-violent war in history when Gandhi led a war of independence against Britain in which he refused to allow any violence.

The reasons why they believe in non-violence are:

- the Hindu belief of ahimsa or non-violence is one of the moral codes of Hinduism;

- connected with ahimsa is the belief that to take life will darken the soul and put it further back on the way to moksha;

- Gandhi's idea of satyagraha (truth force) showed that pacifism can work as a way of removing injustice;

- the evidence of wars seems to show that they solve very little.

2 The Hindu Just War

Perhaps the majority of Hindus believe that war is justified if fought in self-defence or to remove great injustice. India has an army which is fighting to keep Kashmir in India, and which fought to protect the Bangladeshis when they were being attacked by Pakistan. The Law of Manu sets out strict rules about war: civilians, women and children must not be harmed; anyone who surrenders, is disarmed or wounded must not be attacked; weapons must be such as to not cause unnecessary suffering (barbed, blazing or poisoned arrows are banned).

The reasons for this view are:

- in the caste system of Hinduism the second most important caste is the warrior caste whose caste duty was to defend society by war if necessary;

- the most popular Hindu holy book, the Bhagavad Gita, says that warriors must fight in just wars and that they need not fear killing because it is only the body that is killed, the soul cannot be harmed;

- there are many stories of battles in the Hindu Scriptures and Rama, the avatar of Vishnu, fought and killed the tyrant king Ravana.

So Hindus have a similar problem to Christians. Most probably accept the need to fight just wars, but a substantial minority is opposed to war in any form.

> Prepare for war with peace in thy soul. Be in peace in pleasure and pain, in gain and in loss, in victory or in the loss of a battle. In this peace there is no sin.

Bhagavad Gita 2:38

> Non-violence is not a garment to be put on and off at will. Its seat is in the heart, and it must be an inseparable part of our being.

Gandhi

Gandhi refused to use violence.

In non-violence, the masses have a weapon which enables a child, a woman, or even a decrepit old man to resist the mightiest government successfully.

Gandhi.

Think thou also of thy duty and do not waver. There is no greater good for a warrior than to fight in a righteous war. There is war that opens up the gates of heaven, Arjuna! Happy the warrior whose fate is to fight such a war.

Bhagavad Gita 2:31–32

Hindu soldiers use the teachings of the Gita to justify fighting in war.

A RELIGIOUS GROUP WORKING FOR WORLD PEACE

Pax Christi was founded by Roman Catholic Christians in France in 1945 to promote reconciliation between French and German Catholics after the violence of the Second World War. Now Pax Christi International has groups dedicated to peace and non-violence in 22 countries on four continents and has consultative status at the United Nations.

Pax Christi USA is the national Catholic peace movement of the United States. It was founded in 1972 as the USA branch of Pax Christi International and is dedicated to reflecting the Peace of Christ (pax Christi is Latin for the peace of Christ) in the life of the American people and witnessing the call of Christians to non-violence. It is one of the most active Pax Christi groups and receives considerable support from the Catholic Bishops of the USA.

The main activities of the group are:

- making public statements about war such as condemning the renewed bombing of Iraq, condemning the airstrikes against Serbia, denouncing military action in the Sudan;

- criticising the American government over issues such as the defence budget and the use of the death penalty;

- organising public debates on issues such as the morality of nuclear weapons;

- working for economic and racial justice to remove the causes of war.

- working for global recognition of human rights;

- educating American Catholics about war and peace issues;

- trying to establish international intervention teams to prevent wars.

Many Christians think the West is wrong to keep bombing Iraq.

Further up-to-date information on the work of Pax Christi USA can be found on http://www.paxchristiusa.org/

Pax Christi USA strives to create a world that reflects the peace of Christ by exploring, articulating and witnessing to the call of Christian non-violence. This work begins in personal life and extends to communities of reflection and action to transform structures of society. Pax Christi USA rejects war, preparations for war and every form of violence and domination. It advocates primacy of conscience, economic and social justice and respect for creation.

The Pax Christi statement of purpose to which all members have to agree.

75 US Catholic Bishops Condemn Policy of Nuclear Deterrence

We come to you, compassionate God, carrying in our hearts men and women who need your gifts of love, wisdom and courage: Bill Clinton, Saddam Hussein, Tarik Aziz, Madeleine Albright, Richard Butler and their associates who participate in their decision making. Speak to them, give them hearts that can hear both you and the cries of the poor as you hear them ... As for ourselves, we confess how often we have been silent while those considered our enemies were attacked. Forgive us for the times our hearts have been cold as they suffered. We ask above all else that you help us respond in the way we have been shown by your son, Jesus. We ask now for compassion and courage to act on behalf of our sisters and brothers in Iraq.

Part of a Pax Christi prayer for peace.

BULLYING

Bullying is intimidating or frightening people who are weaker than yourself. Most people connect bullying with school where children are often picked on by groups of older or stronger children. Such bullying can result in injury, mental illness, suicide or murder.

Other forms of bullying can take place among adults. There is growing evidence of people being bullied at work. Such bullying is normally carried out by managers or supervisors who use their position of power and authority to frighten or humiliate workers who are under their control. Such bullying does not cause physical injury (unlike much school bullying), but can lead to stress, nervous breakdown or even suicide.

Religious attitudes to bullying

All religions see bullying as wrong because:

- all religions see using violence without a just cause as sinful, and bullying always involves using violence (whether physical or verbal) which is unjustified;

- all religions see human beings as individuals who are important because they are a creation of God. Christians and Jews would see bullying as wrong because they believe that every individual has been made in the image of God;

- religious people also see it as their duty to protect the people who are being bullied because all religions teach that protecting the innocent is fulfilling God's will.

Particular reasons for religious people opposing bullying can be seen in the quotation boxes.

Non-religious attitudes to bullying

Bullying is not approved of by society and the law tries to protect the victims of bullying. All schools have to have an anti-bullying policy which should be communicated to all students. All students should be encouraged to report immediately any act of bullying. All trade unions have procedures for workers who are being bullied at work.

The law treats verbal bullying as assault and any bullying which results in physical injury as aggravated assault or causing grievous bodily harm, both of which carry prison sentences.

Society disapproves of bullying because:

- in a democracy, every person has human rights, including the right to be able to live free from fear;

- bullying has harmful effects on society. The victims of bullying are likely to be prevented from achieving their career aims, and therefore the contribution to society they are capable of. The bullies are likely to go on bullying and preventing even more people from making their contribution to society;

- a civilised society is based on the rule of law and mutual respect between the members of that society. Both of these are threatened by the power of bullies.

> Do not defraud your neighbour or rob him. Do not hold back the wages of a hired man overnight. Do not curse the deaf or put a stumbling block in front of the blind, but fear your God, I am the Lord ... Do not go about spreading slander among your people. Do not do anything that endangers your neighbour's life. I am the Lord.

Leviticus 19:13–16

> This is the message you heard from the beginning: We should love one another. Do not be like Cain who belonged to the evil one and murdered his brother. And why did he murder him? Because his own actions were evil and his brother's were righteous... Anyone who hates his brother is a murderer, and you know that no murderer has eternal life in him.

1 John 3:11–15

BLUNKETT ACTS TO ELIMINATE BULLYING

David Blunkett urged schoolchildren not to 'suffer in silence' yesterday as he unveiled advice to schools on how to stop bullying.

In the new guidance, the Education Secretary encouraged head teachers to set up 'peer mentoring' schemes where children acted as counsellors to younger children and urged them not to ignore bullying outside the school gates.

It is believed that up to a million children a year are bullied with up to a third of girls and a quarter of boys afraid to go to school as a result. About ten cases each year end in suicide. Damilola Taylor, the ten-year-old boy who died after complaining of bullying at school in Peckham, has recently brought the issue to light.

The Times, 14 December 2000.

David Blunkett, the Minister of Education, set up measures to stop bullying in schools.

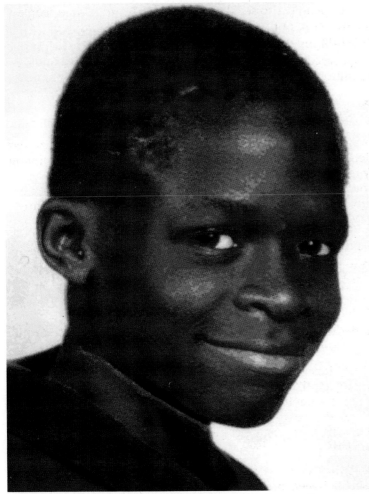

Damilola Taylor was murdered on his way home from school.

Let there arise out of you a band of people inviting to all that is good, enjoining what is right, and forbidding what is wrong: they are the ones to attain felicity. Be not like those who are divided among themselves and fall into disputations after receiving clear signs: for them is a dreadful penalty.

Qur'an 3: 104–105

The principle of ahimsa does not include any evil thought, any unjustified haste, any lies, hatred, ill-will towards anyone.

Mahatma Gandhi

CAUSES OF CONFLICT BETWEEN FAMILIES AND FRIENDS

Family strife began in Coronation Street when a father began an affair.

Conflict does not only occur in wars or bullying. Conflict with friends or family can have devastating effects on people's lives. A conflict between friends can cause the end of a friendship with all the loss, anxiety and guilt that can entail. Conflict within a family can lead to the violence of battered wives or husbands, different groups in the family refusing to have anything to do with each other etc.

Obviously there are many causes of conflict between families and friends; here are some you could use in the examination:

- jealousy because of financial or job success e.g. winning the lottery;

- parents refusing to accept a child's choice of partner;

- disagreements over caring for aged parents;

- disagreements over the contents of wills;

- disagreements over moral issues e.g. a friend or child deciding to cohabit rather than marry; a friend deciding to have an abortion.

Religion sees forgiveness and reconciliation as the way to deal with conflicts between families and friends.

Neighbours go to court over hedge

Young wife only married for money say children contesting will

Who Wants to be a Millionaire winner refuses to reward friend whose answer made £250,000

Parents refuse to attend daughter's wedding to African

Christianity is based on the concept of forgiveness and reconciliation. Most Christians believe that humanity had become split from God through sin, but the forgiveness of sins brought by the death of God's son, Jesus, has allowed reconciliation between God and humans. Christianity teaches that Christians should be committed to forgiveness and reconciliation when there are conflicts between families or friends. Christians believe that the power of forgiveness and love can lead to reconciliation and the ending of conflict.

Christians believe they should forgive and try to bring reconciliation because:

- Jesus died on the cross to bring forgiveness and reconciliation;

- when Peter asked if he should forgive his brother up to seven times, Jesus told him that he should forgive up to 77 times;

- Jesus said that if people do not forgive those who have sinned against them, God will not forgive their sins;

- St Paul said that Christians should try to live in peace with everyone.

However, Christians would say that if the quarrel is about a religious or moral issue and the person quarrelled with is going against Christian beliefs, then there can be no reconciliation. Christian beliefs should not be given up for either friends or family.

The crucifixion by Craigie Aitchison (1959).

CHRISTIANITY AND FORGIVENESS

> Then Peter came to Jesus and asked, 'Lord, how many times shall I forgive my brother when he sins against me? Up to seven times?' Jesus answered, 'I tell you not seven times, but seventy-seven times.'

Matthew 18:21–22

> And when you stand praying, if you hold anything against anyone, forgive him, so that your Father in heaven may forgive you your sins.

Mark 11:26

> If anyone has caused grief ... you ought to forgive and comfort him.

2 Corinthians 2:7

> Forgiveness also bears witness that, in our world, love is stronger than sin. The martyrs of yesterday and today bear witness to Jesus. Forgiveness is the fundamental condition of the reconciliation of the children of God with their Father and of men with one another.

Catechism of the Catholic Church.

ISLAM AND FORGIVENESS

Islam teaches that God is merciful and that those who truly repent of their sins will be forgiven. Consequently, Muslims should be forgiving to those who cause them offence. Muslims believe that they should be forgiving because:

- God is Compassionate and Merciful to sinners, and so Muslims should be merciful and forgiving;

- on the Day of Judgement God will deal with everyone as they deserve, but Muslims will be able to request his mercy. However, how can Muslims ask for God's forgiveness if they are not prepared to forgive?

- the Qur'an says that Muslims should forgive other people's sins against them and Muslims should obey the Qur'an as they believe it is the word of God;

- there are many hadith from the Prophet Muhammad about forgiving people who have offended others and Muslims believe they should follow the example of the Prophet.

Nevertheless, Muslims should not forgive those who are working against Islam, or those who are denying Muslim principles.

> **The recompense for an injury is an injury equal thereto in degree; but if a person forgives and makes reconciliation, his reward is due from God.**
>
> *Surah 42:40*

> **If anyone does evil or wrongs his own soul, but afterwards seeks God's forgiveness, he will find God Oft-forgiving, Most Merciful.**
>
> *Surah 4:110*

> **Be forgiving and control yourself in the face of provocation; give justice to the person who was unfair and unjust to you; give to the one who did not help you when you were in need, and keep fellowship with the one who did not care about you.**
>
> *Hadith*

> **A kind word with forgiveness is better than charity followed by injury.**
>
> *Surah 2:263*

Muslims use calligraphy as decoration and it often reminds them that Allah is Compassionate and Merciful.

JUDAISM AND FORGIVENESS

The Yom Kippur service encourages forgiveness.

> So they sent word to Joseph saying, 'Your father left these instructions before he died: "This is what you are to say to Joseph: I ask you to forgive your brothers the sins and wrongs they committed in treating you so badly."'
>
> *Genesis 50:16–17*

> You are forgiving and good, O Lord, abounding in love to all who call to you.
>
> *Psalm 86:5*

Judaism teaches that Jews should forgive those who wrong them. In the ten days between Rosh Hashanah and Yom Kippur, Jews are expected to seek out anyone they have wronged and ask their forgiveness. They do this because on Yom Kippur, they are going to ask God to forgive them for all the wrongs they have done to God in the past year. Jews believe they should be forgiving because:

- God forgives those who turn to him in true repentance;
- the Tenakh encourages Jews to forgive those who wrong them;
- the rabbis encourage Jews to forgive those who wrong them;
- Jews always try to forgive those who have wronged them when on their deathbed, before they ask God to forgive their sins.

However, Jews are not expected to forgive those who do not ask for forgiveness nor are they expected to forgive the enemies of Judaism.

> Judaism is very clear that God cannot forgive you any sin against someone else if you have not tried to put things right yourself.
>
> *Judaism*, C. M. Pilkington.

> And so may it be Your will, Lord our God and God of our fathers, to have mercy on us and forgive us all our sins, grant us atonement for our iniquities, and forgive and pardon us for all transgressions.
>
> From the prayers for Yom Kippur.

HINDUISM AND FORGIVENESS

Some Hindus do not believe in forgiveness as they think that everyone suffers according to their previous lives. Whatever happens is a result of people's karma and forgiveness does not come into the matter.

> When a man sees all beings within his very self, and his self within all beings ... he has reached the seed – without body or wound, without sinews, not riddled by evil.

Isa Upanishad 6–8

> Even if someone attacks you with abuses, insults and beatings for no reason, do not be harsh to them. Bear and endure them. Forgive and bless your tormentors.

Shiksapatri 202

Hiindu swamis encourage forgiveness of others to free the soul.

> According as one acts, according as one conducts oneself, so does one become. The doer of good becomes good. The doer of evil becomes evil. One becomes virtuous by virtuous action, bad by bad action.

Brhadaranyaka Upanishad 4.4.5

Many Hindus believe that it is wrong to hold bitter thoughts about people who have wronged them and think that it is better for one's soul to forgive those who have committed the wrong. They believe this because:

- the belief in the gunas means that forgiveness is a quality of light (sattva) whereas hatred and bitterness are part of the forces of dark (tamas) which keep the soul from moksha;

- the Upanishads teach the danger to the soul of not forgiving those who seek your forgiveness;

- many swamis have taught that to forgive those who have wronged a person is part of the process of liberating the soul (moksha).

QUESTIONS

Factfile 20 War and peace issues

1 Name two weapons of mass destruction.

2 Choose one conflict in the world and explain why the conflict is happening.

Factfile 21 Christianity and war

1 What is pacifism?

2 Explain why some Christians believe they should be pacifists.

3 Give a Christian definition of a just war.

4 Explain why some Christians believe they can fight in just wars.

Factfiles 22, 23, 24 Islam, Judaism and Hinduism and war

1 Choose one religion other than Christianity and explain what is needed for its followers to fight in a war.

2 What reasons do they have for their attitude to war?

3 'It is an insult to God for people to spend billions on weapons when people are starving.'
Do you agree? Give reasons for your opinion, showing that you have considered another point of view. In your answer, you should refer to at least one religion.

Factfile 25 A religious group working for world peace

1 Give an outline of the work of one religious organisation working for world peace.

2 Explain why they do this work.

Factfile 26 Bullying

1 State three effects of bullying.

2 Have a class discussion on how bullying can be prevented.

Factfile 27 Causes of conflict between family and friends

1 What are the main causes of conflict between families?

2 What are the main causes of conflict between friends?

Factfile 28 Christianity and forgiveness

1 Give an outline of Christian teaching on forgiveness.

2 Explain why Christians may be forced to argue with their family.

Factfiles 29, 30, 31 Islam, Judaism and Hinduism and forgiveness

1 Choose one religion other than Christianity and give an outline of its teaching on forgiveness.

2 'Religious people should never argue with their families.'
Do you agree? Give reasons for your opinion, showing that you have considered another point of view. In your answer, you should refer to at least one religion.

SIN – AN ACT AGAINST THE WILL OF GOD.

CRIME – AN ACT AGAINST THE LAW.

LAW – RULES MADE BY PARLIAMENT AND ENFORCEABLE BY THE COURTS.

JUSTICE – DUE ALLOCATION OF REWARD AND PUNISHMENT, THE MAINTENANCE OF WHAT IS RIGHT.

DETERRENCE – THE IDEA THAT PUNISHMENTS SHOULD BE OF SUCH A NATURE THAT THEY WILL PUT PEOPLE OFF (DETER) COMMITTING CRIMES.

RETRIBUTION – THE IDEA THAT PUNISHMENTS SHOULD MAKE CRIMINALS PAY FOR WHAT THEY HAVE DONE WRONG.

REFORM – THE IDEA THAT PUNISHMENTS SHOULD TRY TO CHANGE CRIMINALS SO THEY WILL NOT COMMIT CRIMES AGAIN.

JUDGEMENT – THE ACT OF JUDGING PEOPLE AND THEIR ACTIONS.

PUNISHMENT – A PENALTY GIVEN FOR ANY CRIME OR OFFENCE.

CAPITAL PUNISHMENT – THE DEATH PENALTY FOR A CRIME OR OFFENCE.

FACTFILE 32
LAW AND JUSTICE

Laws are rules about how to behave whilst justice is about rewarding the good and punishing the bad and making sure that what is right is what happens in society. In the United Kingdom, laws are passed by Parliament (see flow chart) and justice is given by the courts (see diagram).

Law and justice are not always the same thing as can be seen by looking at the difference between a sin and a crime. A sin is an act against the will of God, but it will not necessarily be a crime, though it will often be unjust. For example it is not a crime for a millionaire to refuse to give food to a starving person, but it is a sin and it is not just.

A crime is an activity that breaks the law of the land and which is subject to official punishment, but it will not necessarily be a sin, and it will not necessarily be unjust. For example, Martin Luther King committed crimes in his civil disobedience campaign to gain civil rights for black Americans in the 1960s. It was a crime to sit on a seat reserved for white people, but it was not a sin and the law itself was unjust.

Christian leaders such as Martin Luther King encourage Christians to challenge the law if it is unjust.

Why do we need laws?

Human beings live in groups, and any group needs rules to organise the behaviour of individuals and to protect the weak from the strong. Imagine what the roads would be like if there were no laws: people would be able to drive on whichever side of the road they liked; people would be able to drive at any speed they liked; there could be no traffic lights because drivers would not need to obey them. Imagine what it would be like if there were no business laws: people could take the money for selling a house and then not move; people could be sacked for no reason and given no compensation. Imagine what life would be like if there were no laws on stealing, murder, rape … .

Society needs laws so that:

- people know what sort of behaviour to expect from each other;
- people can work and be involved in business without someone taking away all the rewards of their work;
- people are protected from violence.

Why does there need to be a connection between the law and justice?

St Thomas Aquinas said that an unjust law is not a proper law. This is because:

- if a law is unjust people will feel that it is right to break the law;
- if some laws are unjust, people may start to think that all laws are unjust;
- if a law does not give justice to people, people will take the law into their own hands.

The Old Bailey is the most famous Crown Court in the United Kingdom.

No arts; no letters; no society; and what is worst of all, continual fear and danger of violent death; and the life of man solitary, poor, nasty, brutish and short.

Thomas Hobbes saying what life would be like without laws in his book *Leviathan*.

How laws are made in the United Kingdom

A bill is introduced into the House of Commons by the government or an MP (Private Member's Bill) and given its First Reading

↓

The Bill is then seriously debated in its Second Reading

↓

The Bill is analysed by a committee of the House of Commons and sent back for

↓

the Third Reading in the House of Commons when the Bill is voted on and, if passed, sent to the House of Lords

↓

The Bill is debated in the House of Lords and normally passed (the Lords can only reject a Bill passed by the Commons three times after which it automatically goes for

↓

Royal Assent – when the Bill is passed by the Lords the Monarch signs it and it becomes law (an Act of Parliament).

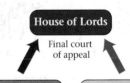

House of Lords
Final court of appeal

Court of appeal (civil) | **Court of appeal (criminal)**

High Court
Deals with claims over £10 000 – libel, tax, family law, etc.

Crown Court
Judge and jury for indictable offences

Magistrates Court
Deals with committal proceedings for Crown Courts, less serious criminal cases, traffic offences, marital disputes, public house licences, etc.

County Court
Deals with small claims, straight-forward adoption, divorce, custody

Civil Law
For settling disputes between individuals

Criminal Law
For dealing with criminal acts

CHRISTIANITY AND JUSTICE

Justice has always been an important issue in Christianity. Christians believe that God is just and will reward the good and punish the evil, if not in this life, then in the world to come. They also believe that God wants the world to be ruled justly and so they believe that Christians should be concerned about fairness. As part of their belief in justice, Christians believe they should work for a fairer sharing of the earth's resources; the removal of poor country debts to rich country governments and banks; the guarantee of basic human rights.

The Christian Churches were the instigators of the Jubilee 2000 campaign to persuade the governments of the rich countries to cancel the debts of poor countries as they believed it was unjust to force poor countries to pay up to 80 per cent of their income in interest payments on the debts they accumulated in the 1970s.

Christian attitudes to justice can be seen in the fact that Exeter Cathedral has a special chapel for justice and peace. In its programme for the year 2000, special events were organised on behalf of: The fellowship of Reconciliation/Peace Care, the Devon Forum for Justice, the Devon Christian Ecology Group, Christian Aid/CAFOD, the Exeter Volunteer bureau, the Cyprus and the Gulf Liaison Group, the World Development Team, HM Prison Exeter, the Devon HIV/AIDS Association. This shows how Christian concern for justice covers every aspect of life where there might be unfairness.

> **And there is no God apart from me, a just God and a saviour.**
>
> *Isaiah 45:21*

> **Blessed are those who hunger and thirst for righteousness.**
>
> *Matthew 5:6*

> **Anyone who does not do what is right (just) is not a child of God; nor is anyone who does not love his brother.**
>
> *1 John 3:10*

The Chapel of Justice in Exeter Cathedral.

The World Council of Churches Assembly, at Vancouver in 1984, invited Christian communities across the world to engage in a process of 'Justice, peace and the integrity of creation'. This was renewed at the Assembly in Canberra in 1991 and the Assembly in Harare in 1998.

Christians believe in justice because:

- the Bible says that God is a God of justice;

- the Bible says that people should be treated fairly and not cheated;

- Jesus said that the rich should share with the poor;

- there are many statements in the New Testament about how Christians should treat people fairly and equally;

- the Churches have made many statements about the need for Christians to work for justice and fairness in the world.

NB In the Bible, the words justice and righteousness are used as if they were the same word (synonymously).

Christians should campaign for policies that reflect Justice, Peace and the wholeness of Creation by:
- promoting laws that do not discriminate against people who are financially less well-off;
- addressing the urgent issues of human population control, hunger and famine;
- encouraging more openness between people of different faiths and cultures;
- working for disarmament and the conversion of arms manufacturing to other uses.

From a pamphlet of the Exeter Diocesan Board for Christian Care.

Inside the Chapel of Justice.

Thank you God, for the freedom to raise my voice in protest. Thank you God, that I can stand with poor people and make a difference. Thank you God, that your love and justice still grab the headlines and make the news. Thank you God, that I belong to a global community working for a fairer world for all people.

Christian Aid prayer.

ISLAM AND JUSTICE

Muslims believe that God is a just God who will reward the good and punish the bad on the Last Day. Muslims believe that it is part of their role as vice-gerents of God's creation to behave justly to other people and to ensure that the world is governed in a fair way. For Islam, the way to do this is to follow the Shari'ah. In Islam the law of the land should be the law of God, the Shari'ah, and so Islam has always had a system of justice based on courts with strict rules about how everyone should be treated fairly by the courts.

As part of their belief in justice, Muslims refuse to be involved in the charging of interest. They believe that interest is unjust because it takes money from the poor and gives it to the rich whereas the just thing would be to take money from the rich and give it to the poor.

> **O ye who believe! Stand out firmly for justice, as witnesses to God, even as against yourselves or your parents, or your kin, and whether it be against rich or poor.**
>
> *Surah 4:135*

ISLAMIC INVESTMENT BANKING UNIT

Serving the Muslim community today...and even better tomorrow.

Islamic Investment Banking Unit 7 Baker Street, London W1M 1AB

The Islamic Investment Banking Unit is here for you. For some time now we've been offering financial assistance to Muslims who wish to buy homes in a way that complies with Islamic Sharia'a.

Our Manzil Home Purchase Plans have proved a very popular choice.

But this is just the start.

We're working to introduce many more products especially designed for you. Our goal is to give Muslims in the U.K. the opportunity to conduct all their financial affairs in a manner consistent with their faith. Insha'Allah, you'll be hearing much more from us in the year to come.

For more information, please contact Waheed Qaiser, Head of UK Islamic Business on our freephone number **0800 783 3323**
Or visit our new website at **www.iibu.com**

Written information about the terms on which IIBU is prepared to do business in relation to Manzil for a specific transaction are available on request. Your home is at risk if you do not keep up your repayments on a mortgage, other loan or facility secured on it. IIBU is a segregated division of The United Bank of Kuwait PLC, British bank regulated by the Financial Services Authority (FSA) and Investment Management Regulatory Organisation (IMRO).

> **Say, 'My Lord hath commanded justice.'**
>
> *Surah 7:29*

> **And the firmament has He raised high, and He has set up the balance of justice in order that ye may not transgress.**
>
> *Surah 55:7*

Muslims believe that all people should have equal rights before the law and that Muslims should work for a fairer sharing of the earth's resources. The pillar of zakah and the work of groups such as Muslim Aid and Islamic Relief are all trying to bring justice into the world.

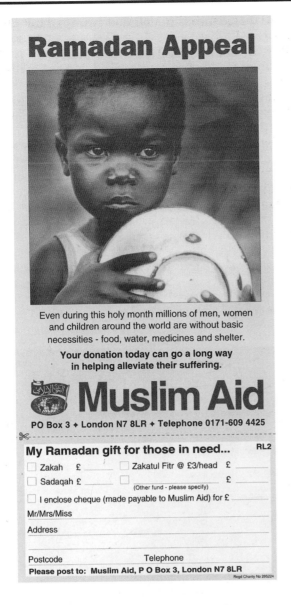

Ramadan Appeal

Even during this holy month millions of men, women and children around the world are without basic necessities - food, water, medicines and shelter.

Your donation today can go a long way in helping alleviate their suffering.

Muslim Aid

PO Box 3 ✦ London N7 8LR ✦ Telephone 0171-609 4425

✂ -

My Ramadan gift for those in need...   RL2

☐ Zakah   £ _____   ☐ Zakatul Fitr @ £3/head   £ _____

☐ Sadaqah £ _____   ☐ _____   £ _____
                      (Other fund - please specify)

☐ I enclose cheque (made payable to Muslim Aid) for £ _____

Mr/Mrs/Miss _____

Address _____

_____

Postcode _____ Telephone _____

Please post to: Muslim Aid, P O Box 3, London N7 8LR

Regd Charity No 295224

Boraidah reported that the Prophet said: Judges are of three kinds: One kind will be in Paradise and two in Hell. As for one who will be inParadise, he is a man who recognises truth and gives a decree accordingly, and a man who recognises truth but is unjust in decree is in Hell, and a man who passes a decree for the people out of ignorance is in Hell.

Hadith quoted by Abu Daud.

In the administration of justice there shall be no distinction between the strangers and relatives, between the Muslim and non-Muslim, and between the high and low. All stand equal in the eye of the Islamic law of justice.

Nisar Ahmed, *The Fundamental Teachings of Qur'an and Hadith.*

Muslims believe in justice because:

- the Qur'an describes God as just;
- the Qur'an says that God wants people to treat each other fairly and to establish justice;
- there are many hadith in which Muhammad is shown as acting justly and/or telling Muslims to treat everyone justly;
- the Shari'ah is based on justice for everyone;
- everyone is equal before Islamic law;
- the pillar of zakah is based on the concept of justice;
- Islamic teaching on the Last Day is concerned with the need for the good to be rewarded and the evil punished which is the basis of justice.

Zakat creates love and brotherhood between the rich and the poor, it minimises social tension and bridges the gap between them and it provides social and economic security for the whole society. Those who are blessed can thus see their wealth as a trust from Allah to Whom it truly belongs. And they can therefore fulfil the goal towards social justice.

Islamic Relief Zakat Guide.

JUDAISM AND JUSTICE

Jews believe that justice is tremendously important. God is just, and God created the world as a place of justice and so Jews must practise justice themselves. From the earliest times, Judaism has had a system of justice and courts based on the Torah. Jews have to live their lives according to the mitzvot (laws) of the Torah and so it has always been important for the courts to operate fairly and for everyone to be treated equally by the law.

As part of their belief in justice, Jews have been very involved in the struggle for equal rights and the change of unjust laws. Many American Jews felt it was their duty to join the civil rights movement led by the Christian, Martin Luther King, which campaigned for equal rights for black Americans in the 1960s. Anatoly Scharansky, a Jewish Soviet scientist, campaigned for human rights in the USSR.

Most Jews also believe that they should work for a fairer sharing of the earth's resources because God's justice applies to the whole world, not simply the Jewish people. Consequently, Jews are involved in groups such as Oxfam as well as World Jewish Relief.

> Oh, praise the greatness of our God! He is the Rock, his works are perfect and all his ways are just. A faithful God who does no wrong, upright and just is he.

Deuteronomy 32:3–4

Anatole Scharansky, a leading scientist who campaigned for equal rights for Jews in the USSR.

Jews believe in justice because:

- the Torah says that God is a God of justice;
- the Tenakh says that people should be treated fairly and not cheated;
- the Tenakh, Talmud and rabbis say that the rich should share with the poor;
- there are many statements in the Responsa about how Jews should treat people fairly and equally.

Amos 5:14–15

World Jewish Relief sends medical and food aid to bring justice to the people of Bosnia.

Seven ways of giving charity, each one better than the last

1 to give sadly;
2 to give less than is suitable, but cheerfully;
3 to give only after being asked;
4 to give before being asked;
5 to give in such a way that the recipient does not know who gave it;
6 to give in such a way that neither knows who the other is;
7 not to give charity, but to take the poor into business partnerships or lend them money so that they can improve their situation without any loss of self-respect.

Jewish Values – Maimonides.

Pray for the welfare of the government; if it were not for the fear of it, men would swallow each other alive.

Ethics of the Fathers.

The Talmud tells the story of a Jewish rabbi who was helped into a boat by a man. When he was aboard the boat, the man told him that he was to appear before him in the court in the near future. The rabbi disqualified himself from the case because he might not be fair since the man had helped him.

Adapted from the *Talmud*.

HINDUISM AND JUSTICE

> **Who have all the powers of their soul in harmony, and the same loving mind for all; who find joy in the good of all beings – they reach in truth my very self.**

Bhagavad Gita 12:4

> May all be happy here;
> May all be free from disease.
> May all be righteous
> and without suffering.

Hindu prayer.

> Manu is quite specific about the moral retribution due to action over a period of lives ... Mental actions such as coveting the possessions of others, thinking about what is undesirable and believing in false ideas; verbal actions such as lying, abuse, slander and gossip; and bodily actions such as theft, violence which is against the law and adultery, all result in a specific kind of retribution in a future life.

Themes and Issues in Hinduism, P Bowen.

> If you happen to be in power as the chief of state executive, then live a righteous religious life, treat your subjects like members of your family, take good care of them and make an honest attempt to consolidate morality and religion in your state.

Shikshapatri of Lord Swaminarayan.

The Hindu concept of justice is based on the belief in dharma. Dharma means the religious, social and moral duties which Hindus must perform if they are to gain moksha (liberation from rebirth). For many Hindus, justice also includes the belief in ahimsa (non-violence) and sattya (truth).

For most Hindus this means that they should try to promote justice in terms of: treating all people as equals; making sure that there is freedom of religion; making sure that everyone has equal political rights. It also means that Hindus should work for a fairer sharing of wealth and the earth's resources. The exploitation of the poor by the rich is a form of violence and ignores the truth that society can only be happy if all the members of that society have a basic standard of living.

Mahatma Gandhi based his campaign for the independence of India from British rule on the Hindu idea of justice. He also developed the idea of sarvodaya (welfare for all) from the Hindu concept of justice. Gandhi's followers since independence have tried to put these beliefs into practice by campaigning for: a fairer distribution of land, equal rights for dalits (people outside the caste system) and women.

Hindus are concerned to bring justice to all the people of India.

Hindus believe in justice because:

- the Hindu goal of life is to gain moksha which requires Hindus to fulfil their dharma which involves justice;

- the Hindu scriptures, especially the *Bhagavad Gita*, encourage Hindus to be concerned for others and to work for justice;

- great Hindu leaders, such as Gandhi, have campaigned for justice and tried to make India a more just society;

- Hindu gurus and swamis teach that people's souls are improved if they treat other people justly.

Some Hindus, however, feel that justice comes from the caste system and the law of karma which involves different treatment of high and low caste members. They believe that this unequal system is justice because it is rewarding the good (on the basis of what they did in their previous lives) and punishing the evil (on the basis of what they did in their previous lives).

THE NATURE OF PUNISHMENT

Many people think prisons should treat criminals very harshly to make people frightened of being sent to prison.

If a society has laws, it must also have punishments for those who break the laws. The main aim of punishment is to try to make sure that everyone obeys the law. However, there are several other theories about what punishment should do.

Retribution
Many people think that the punishment should make criminals pay for their crime in proportion to the severity of the crime they have committed. In the past such retributive punishments would have killed those who committed murder and taken the eyes out of those who blinded someone. Nowadays, those who believe in retribution think that criminals should suffer for what they have done wrong.

Deterrence
Many people think that punishment should be very severe to deter people from committing crimes. For example, if someone knows they will have their hand cut off if they are caught stealing, then they will not steal; if people know they will be executed if they are caught murdering, they will not murder.

Reform
Many people think that punishment should be aimed at reforming the criminal so that they become honest law-abiding citizens who will not want to commit crimes again. Reformative punishments often involve giving criminals education and qualifications so that they do not feel the need to be a criminal.

Protection
Many people feel that society must be protected from violent people or persistent burglars, so punishments should put such criminals in prison where they are no longer a danger to society.

Most forms of punishment are a mixture of theories. For example, imprisonment can deter, protect, inflict retribution and give reformation through education, training and counselling.

Drug Dealer freed for saving man

A convicted drugs dealer has had 14 days removed from his 30-month prison sentence for saving a motorcyclist's life. The prisoner was on his way to hospital when prison officers stopped at a road accident and allowed him to use the first aid skills he had learnt in prison to stop the man from bleeding to death.

The Times, 8 November 2000.

I don't believe children are born evil. I have probably seen 350 young people come through and every one has had an experience which has led to their criminal activity. One lad was made to live in a kennel, another had bleach poured over him to make him white, another was shackled to keep him in. A girl in here has arms like pork crackling from cutting herself. They often come in filthy; many of them have never had their teeth cleaned. It upsets me that people don't have empathy with these children. They don't know what they have been through.

Statement from the head of education in a secure unit for young offenders which tries to reform young teenagers who have committed very serious crimes.

CHRISTIANITY AND PUNISHMENT

Jesus seems to have regarded punishment as something which belongs to God, not humans. Consequently, many Christians believe that the only purpose of punishment is to reform criminals. They believe that no one is irredeemable and that, as it is possible to be changed by the saving power of God, every criminal should be given the opportunity to repent and reform their lives. They believe this because:

- Jesus said that Christians should not judge other people;

- when Jesus was confronted by the woman caught in adultery who, according to the Jewish law, should have been punished by being stoned to death, he said that only those without any sin should throw a stone;

- Jesus said that Christians should always try to settle their problems without having to use the courts;

- the Church has always looked on itself as a way to bring new life to criminals;

- in the Middle Ages, cathedrals had sanctuary knockers and even murderers chased by the law came under the protection of the Church if they could touch the knocker;

- the modern Church has made many statements about the need for punishment to be used to reform criminals and make them fit to live in society again.

> **Do not judge or you too will be judged. For in the same way as you judge others, you will be judged.**
>
> *Matthew 7:1–2*

> **'If any one of you is without sin, let him be the first to throw a stone at her.' ... At this , those who heard began to go away ...**
>
> **Jesus straightened up and asked her, 'Woman where are they? Has no one condemned you?'**
>
> **'No one sir,' she said.**
>
> **'Then neither do I condemn you,' Jesus declared.**
>
> *John 8:7–11*

The sanctuary knocker at Durham Cathedral dates from the Middle Ages when the Bishop allowed criminals who touched the knocker to leave the country.

However, many Christians also believe that punishment should be used to protect society and deter people from committing crimes as well as reforming them. They believe that society has a right to protect itself from criminals who are trying to destroy it. They believe this because:

- St Paul said that civil authorities have the right to use magistrates to uphold the law;

- without a police force and punishment for criminals, society would collapse;

- Church leaders have made statements saying that society has the right to use punishment to deter people from committing crimes and to protect society from violence and theft;

- Jesus threw the money changers out of the Temple showing that he was prepared to judge and punish people for preventing people from praying.

> I urge then, first of all, that prayers and intercessions be made for everyone – for kings and all those in authority, that we may live peaceful and quiet lives in all godliness and holiness.

1 Timothy 2:1–2

> But I tell you, do not resist an evil person. If someone strikes you on the right cheek, turn to him the other also.

Matthew 5:39

Anne Widdecombe is a Christian politician who thinks punishment should be based on deterrence and retribution.

> Christians recognise that Government has a duty on behalf of society to protect that society from crime for the common good. Those found guilty of breaches of the law may be punished. The punishment will include an element of retribution, but the aim of punishment is not primarily retribution, still less revenge, but the reform and rehabilitation of the offender.

Statement by the Methodist Church in *What the Churches Say* second edition.

> The Salvation Army recognises the need of society to be protected from wrongdoers, especially those willing to use violence, but recognises also the responsibility placed upon society so to regulate itself that the dignity and worth of all persons are made paramount, and that the lowest instincts of men and women are not incited or inflamed.

Statement by the Salvation Army on punishment quoted in *What the Churches Say* second edition.

ISLAM AND PUNISHMENT

> **As to the thief, male or female, cut off his or her hands: a punishment by way of example, from God, for their crime.**
>
> *Surah 5:41*

> **The recompense for an injury is an injury equal thereto in degree: but if a person forgives and makes retribution, his reward is due from God: for God loveth not those who do wrong.**
>
> *Surah 42:40*

> **The woman and the man guilty of adultery and fornication, flog each of them with a hundred stripes: let not compassion move you in their case, in a matter prescribed by God.**
>
> *Surah 24:2*

> **Ayesha reported that the Messenger of Allah said: Verily those who were before you were destroyed because when a noble man from them committed theft, they let him off, and when a workman committed theft from among them, they exempted sentence on him. By Allah, had Fatima, daughter of Muhammad, committed theft, I would have cut off her hand.**
>
> *Hadith* reported in all the authorities.

Islam teaches that criminals should be punished and the Qur'an sets down specific punishments for certain crimes. Muslims should not commit crimes because any crime is a sin against God, and Islam teaches that all sins will be punished on the Last Day.

Muslim attitudes to punishment are based on deterrence and reform. The Qur'an says that thieves should have a hand amputated. The threat of this is believed to deter people from stealing and the actual punishment will reform thieves because they will always be aware of what has happened to them and will therefore not risk it happening again. For many other crimes, the Qur'an gives whipping as the punishment with a set number of lashes laid down – for example adultery is to be punished by 100 lashes.

Imprisonment is used in Muslim countries to protect society from anti-social criminals. It is also possible in Islam for a criminal to pay compensation to the victim, or the victim's family, for certain crimes. This is done as a form of retribution.

Would Islamic punishments deter all criminals?

Muslims have these views on punishment because:

- the Qur'an sets down lashes or amputation for certain crimes, and the Qur'an is the word of God which must be followed;

- whipping and amputation allow the offender to remain in society with their families where, it is believed, they are less likely to re-offend than those who have been sent to prison;

- the idea of deterrence requires very severe punishment to deter – amputation is much more likely to deter thieves than six months in prison;

- the strict punishments are only given as a last resort. Islamic courts investigate all the background to the case and, for example, would not amputate the hand of someone who stole to feed their family.

Jews believe that society has a right to punish those who break its laws. The Torah sets down punishments, such as whipping and stoning to death, for various offences. However, Jews believe that the punishments for offences are not part of the mitzvot. No Jewish country would impose punishments by whipping or stoning today. Rather, Jews would look at the principles behind the laws. The idea of an eye for an eye and a tooth for a tooth is actually a restriction on punishment. It shows that if someone knocks your tooth out, you only have the right to one of their teeth, not to knock all of them out or even to chop off their head. Jews also believe that compensation is better than retribution so that the value of a tooth or the value of an eye should form the basis of the punishment.

Jews see the basic reason for punishment as: deterrence, protection and retribution. The aim of punishment is to protect society from the actions of the anti-social, and, if there is sufficient deterrence, there will be very little crime. Neverthless, Jews would also see reform as a major part of the punishment process as this is likely to prevent crimes in the future.

Jews have these ideas about punishment because:

- the Torah says that criminals should be punished;

- the Torah gives deterrence, protection and retribution as the reasons for punishment;

- society would be likely to collapse if criminals did not face punishment;

- rabbis have always been involved in the Jewish court system and the punishment of offenders (the Bet Din must have at least three rabbis).

JUDAISM AND PUNISHMENT

> But if there is serious injury, you are to take life for life, eye for eye, tooth for tooth, hand for hand, foot for foot, burn for burn, wound for wound, bruise for bruise.

Exodus 21:23–24

> While the Israelites were in the desert, a man was found gathering wood on the Sabbath day. Those who found him gathering wood brought him to Moses and Aaron and the whole assembly, and they kept him in custody because it was not clear what should be done to him.

Numbers 15:34

The Bet Din is the court for British Jews on religious matters.

HINDUISM AND PUNISHMENT

Hindus believe that criminals should be punished. It is part of dharma that society should operate smoothly and that the law should operate fairly. Hindus believe it is the dharma of rulers to implement and uphold the law, and this must include the punishment of those who break the law.

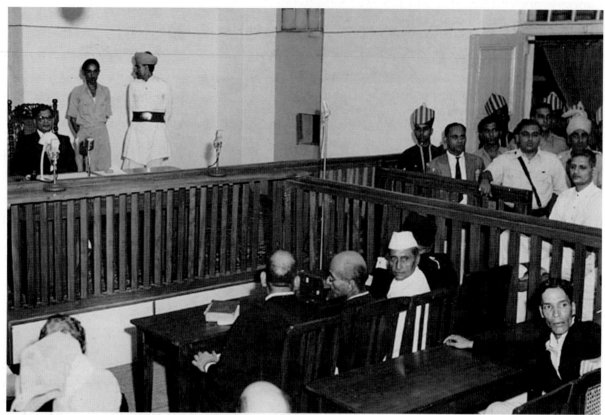

Indian courts work on the same principles as British courts.

Hinduism teaches that everyone has the right to carry out the duties connected with their stage in life. Such duties cannot be carried out if criminals make it impossible to go out of the home in safety or work to support one's family. Consequently, punishment must be used to protect society from criminals, to deter people from committing crimes and to reform those who have committed crimes so that they do not commit crimes again. Most Hindus would feel that punishment should also involve retribution – criminals should pay for what they have done.

Hindus believe in the need for punishment because:

- the Vedas and Upanishads say crime is a sin against the laws of creation and should be punished;

- the Dharma-shastras (ancient Hindu scriptures) give guidelines on punishments for crimes;

- the Mahabharata says that a ruler has a duty to punish criminals;

- the belief in karma means that committing a crime must have the effect of being punished.

You have to study a prisoner of conscience who has been imprisoned for their religious belief. The prisoner can be from the twentieth or twenty-first centuries.

Dietrich Bonhoeffer was a German Christian who was imprisoned and then executed for his religious beliefs by the Nazis.

Born in 1906, Bonhoeffer studied theology (Christian thought) at university in Germany, Rome and New York from 1924 to 1931, after which he became a lecturer and chaplain at Berlin University.

His studies and his experiences as a child during the First World War made him a Christian pacifist, however, as soon as Hitler and the Nazis came to power, Bonhoeffer began to oppose them. He made a broadcast attacking the Nazi idea of leadership only two days after Hitler became Chancellor of Germany and criticised the first Nazi attacks on the Jews in April 1933.

Bonhoeffer was banned from teaching in Berlin and became pastor of two German Lutheran churches in London. Whilst in London he took his two churches out of the control of the Nazi German Church and also made contact with various Church leaders in Britain, including the Archbishop of Canterbury, to tell them the truth about the Nazis. He returned to Germany in 1935 and became head of a training college for student pastors who were opposed to the Nazis. It was here that he was arrested by the Gestapo in 1937.

Hitler was meant to die in the July bomb plot of 1944.

Reasons for the arrest

- Bonhoeffer had made public statements saying that Christians should oppose the Nazi laws on the Jews;

- Bonhoeffer had told the students at the training college that their Christian principles should make them refuse to do military service for the Nazis;

- Bonhoeffer had told Christian leaders around the world that they should have nothing to do with the German Christian Church which was controlled by the Nazis and was the official Protestant Church in Germany;

- Bonhoeffer had preached sermons in Berlin in which he claimed that Christians could not and should not obey laws which contradicted Christian principles;

- Bonhoeffer had had close contacts with Martin Niemuller who was arrested just before Bonhoeffer for his work for Jewish Christians.

> If the leader allows himself to be persuaded by those he leads who want to turn him into an idol ... then the image of the leader will degenerate into a misleader. The leader who makes an idol of himself and his office makes a mockery of God.

Bonhoeffer's radio broadcast in 1933 which was halted by the Nazis.

James Mawdsley's Christian beliefs led to his imprisonment for campaigning for human rights in Burma.

> When the Church sees the state exercising too much or too little law and order, it is its task not simply to bind the wounds of the victims crushed beneath the wheel, but also to put a spoke in the wheel itself.

From a Bonhoeffer sermon.

Effects of the punishment

Bonhoeffer had influential relatives and was only in prison for a few weeks. However, his college was closed down and Bonhoeffer was banned from Berlin except to visit his family.

The effect on Bonhoeffer was to make him realise that pacifism was not going to work with people like the Nazis who could not be opposed by non-violent means. Within weeks of his release, Bonhoeffer had become involved with a group of army officers who were trying to overthrow the Nazis. He decided that it was a Christian's duty when opposed by evil such as Hitler to remove the evil, and so he later became involved in the plots to assassinate Hitler.

In April 1943, Bonhoeffer was arrested on a charge of subverting the armed forces and kept in a Gestapo prison. After the July Bomb Plot of 1944 (when an army officer, von Stauffenberg, planted a bomb at a conference and Hitler was lucky to escape with his life), Gestapo investigations discovered Bonhoeffer's connection with the conspiracy since 1938 and he was moved to Buchenwald concentration camp and executed at Flossenberg extermination camp in April 1945.

Capital punishment is punishment which takes away the criminal's life. This process of judicial killing is called execution or the death penalty. A crime which can be punished by the death penalty is called a capital offence.

In the past offences such as sheep stealing were capital offences, but gradually the number of capital offences was reduced until only murder remained. In 1970, the United Kingdom abolished the death penalty as a form of punishment. There have been debates in Parliament since 1970 on the re-introduction of capital punishment, which have all been defeated.

Non-religious arguments in favour of capital punishment

Those who believe that murder, and often terrorism, should be punished by the death penalty often use the following arguments:

- if people know they will lose their life if they murder someone, it will act as a deterrent and there will be fewer murders;
- murderers and terrorists are a great threat to society, and the best way to protect society from them is to take away their lives so they cannot re-offend;
- human life is the most important thing there is and the value of human life can only be shown by giving those who take human life the worst possible punishment which is the death penalty;
- retribution and/or compensation are major parts of punishment and the only retribution/compensation for taking a life is for the criminal's life to be taken.

Non-religious arguments against capital punishment

Those who argued for the abolition of the death penalty often used the following arguments:

- no court system can be sure that the correct verdict is always given. People are convicted for offences which it is later proved they did not commit;
- the statistics of countries with the death penalty and those without show that, if anything, those countries which do not use the death penalty have a lower murder rate;
- many murderers do not expect to be caught and so do not think about the punishment;
- murderers who know they are going to be killed if caught are more likely to kill more people to avoid being caught;
- terrorists who are executed are hailed as martyrs and encourage more of their followers to become terrorists;
- human life is the most important thing there so no one has the right to take it. Executing murderers demonstrates that society doesn't regard human life as sacred;
- murderers often regard life imprisonment as worse than death and try to commit suicide.

CAPITAL PUNISHMENT

Some countries use death by injection as capital punishment.

CHRISTIANITY AND CAPITAL PUNISHMENT

There are different attitudes among Christians towards capital punishment.

Many Christians believe that capital punishment is un-Christian and can never be justified. They feel that Christians should never be involved in capital punishment and should campaign against its use. They believe this because:

- Christianity is based on the belief that Jesus came to save (reform) sinners. It is impossible to reform a criminal who has been executed;

- Jesus banned retribution when he said that an eye for an eye and a tooth for a tooth is wrong. For Christians, the Law of the New Testament has replaced the Law of the Old Testament which permits capital punishment;

- Christianity teaches that human life is sacred and that only God has the right to take life. If abortion and euthanasia are wrong, then the death penalty must be wrong;

- most of the Christian Churches have condemned capital punishment, and even those which have not, such as the Roman Catholic Church, have groups of leaders which have condemned capital punishment, such as the Catholic Bishops Conference of the USA.

Such Christians would also use all the non-religious arguments against capital punishment.

> **The Laws of the Realm may punish Christian men with death for heinous and grievous offences.**

Article 37 of the Thirty Nine Articles of the Church of England.

> **You have heard that it was said, 'Eye for eye, tooth for tooth.' But I tell you, Do not resist an evil person. If someone strikes you on the right cheek, turn to him the other also.**

Matthew 5:38

10 Rillington Place. Timothy Evans was executed for murders which took place here, but it was later proved that he did not commit them.

Some Christians believe that capital punishment can be used by Christians as the best way of preventing murder and keeping order in society. They believe this because:

- the Bible sets down the death penalty as the punishment for a number of crimes, so it is allowed by God;

- the Roman Catholic Church and the Church of England have not retracted their statements which permit the state to use capital punishment;

- the Christian Church itself used capital punishment in the past for the crime of heresy (holding beliefs different from official Church teachings). This means that capital punishment cannot be un-Christian;

- Christian thinkers such as Thomas Aquinas argued that punishment in Christianity should reform the sinner and secure peace for society. He said that the peace of society is more important than the reform of the sinner, and that Christians can therefore use capital punishment to preserve the peace of society.

Such Christians would also use all the non-religious arguments in favour of capital punishment.

> We do not have the right, even in the case of those who have committed dreadful crimes including the murder of others, to take their lives as punishment. The United Reformed Church believes that even the most depraved person is capable of reform, and that it is society's role to offer that possibility of reform through the systems of confinement and imprisonment which the state organises.

Statement by the United Reform Church quoted in *What the Churches Say*, second edition.

> If a man hates his neighbour and lies in wait for him, assaults and kills him and then flees to one of these cities, the elders of his town shall send for him, bring him back from the city and hand him over to the avenger of blood to die. Show him no pity. You must purge from Israel the guilt of shedding innocent blood.

Deuteronomy 19:11–13

> Do not repay anyone evil for evil. Be careful to do what is right in the sight of everybody ... Do not take revenge, my friends, but leave room for God's wrath, for it is written, 'It is mine to revenge, I will repay.'

Romans 12:17–19

ISLAM AND CAPITAL PUNISHMENT

Islam allows capital punishment for three offences: murder, adultery and apostasy (a Muslim denying Islam and working against Islam). Such crimes must be clearly proven and established by the correct processes of law laid down by the Shari'ah. Muslims agree with capital punishment because:

- it is a punishment set down by God in the Qur'an;

- Muhammad made several statements agreeing with capital punishment for murder, adultery and apostasy;

- Muhammad sentenced people to death for murder when he was ruler of Madinah;

- the Shari'ah says that capital punishment is the punishment for murder, adultery and apostasy.

Muslims would also use the non-religious arguments in favour of capital punishment.

Take not life – which God has made sacred – except for just cause.

Surah 17:33

The shedding of the blood of a Muslim is not lawful except for one of three reasons: a life for a life, a married person who commits adultery and one who turns aside from his religion and abandons the community.

Hadith quoted by Bukhari and Muslim.

Execution is permitted in Muslim States.

For the crime of apostasy, it should be borne in mind that in an Islamic State, Islam is the State, not just the state religion. Any act of apostasy which results in open rebellion against Islam is, therefore, an act of treason. Even in Britain, the penalty for treason is death.

What Does Islam Say? Ibrahim Hewitt.

Some Muslims do not agree with capital punishment because of the non-religious arguments. They feel that capital punishment is recommended by the Qur'an, but is not compulsory.

JUDAISM AND CAPITAL PUNISHMENT

Mass murderers Fred and Rosemary West. He committed suicide rather than serve life imprisonment.

Most Jews believe that capital punishment is acceptable, but should only be used as a last resort and with severe restrictions. Murderers who will not pose a threat to society should not be executed as they have a potential to reform. However, those who are likely to murder again should be executed to protect society. Jews believe this because:

- the Torah says that capital punishment should be used for certain offences;

- the Talmud says that capital punishment is allowed, but only if: the murderer has been warned of the consequences of their action; there are two independent witnesses to the murder;

- the Mishnah says that a Bet Din that executed a person once in 70 years, was a destructive Bet Din.

- the basis of the Jewish theory of punishment is the protection of society, and so capital punishment should be used if a convicted criminal is a threat to society or if capital punishment will deter people from becoming a danger to society.

Such Jews would also use the non-religious arguments in favour of capital punishment.

Some Jews do not believe in capital punishment because of the Mishnah and the non-religious arguments against capital punishment.

> **If anyone takes the life of a human being, he must be put to death. Anyone who takes the life of someone's animal must make restitution – life for life.**
>
> *Leviticus 24:17*

> **On the testimony of two or three witnesses, a man shall be put to death, but no one shall be put to death on the testimony of only one witness.**
>
> *Deuteronomy 17:6*

> **I believe with perfect faith that the Creator, blessed be his name, rewards those who keep his commandments and punishes those who do not.**
>
> Number 11 of the Thirteen Principles of Faith.

HINDUISM AND CAPITAL PUNISHMENT

Most Hindus believe that capital punishment can, and should, be used for convicted murderers. They believe that the death penalty both deters criminals and protects the order of society. They believe this because:

- the Vedas say that ahimsa does not apply to enemies in war or criminals, so both can be lawfully killed;

- the Law of Manu says that it is permitted for a Hindu to kill someone to prevent something worse happening or to maintain social order. This is taken to mean that the execution of murderers is permitted to maintain social order;

- the Varaha Purana says that a king may put a criminal to death to restore the correct dharma to society.

Such Hindus would also use the non-religious arguments in favour of capital punishment.

Some Hindus do not believe in capital punishment because of Gandhi's teaching that ahimsa means no violence to anyone, and also because of the non-religious arguments against capital punishment.

> Take for example, a manacled man brought here by people shouting, 'He's a thief! He has committed a theft! Heat an axe for him!' Now, if he is guilty of the crime, then he turns himself into a lie uttering a falsehood and covering himself in falsehood, he takes hold of the axe and gets burnt upon which he is executed. If, on the other hand, he is innocent of the crime, then he turns himself into the truth; uttering the truth, he takes hold of the axe and is not burnt upon which he is released.

Chandogya Upanishad 6.16.1–2

> If any man thinks he slays, and if another thinks he is slain, neither knows the ways of truth. The Eternal in man cannot kill: the Eternal in man cannot die.

Bhagavad Gita 2:19

QUESTIONS

Factfile 32 Law and justice

1 Give an outline of how new laws are made in the United Kingdom.

2 Explain why it is important to have laws in society.

3 Explain, with appropriate examples, the differences between a sin and a crime.

Factfile 33 Christianity and justice

1 Give an outline of the work of one Christian group which is trying to promote justice.

2 Explain why they do this work.

Factfiles 34, 35, 36 Islam, Judaism and Hinduism and justice

1 Choose one religion other than Christianity and give an outline of its teaching on justice.

2 'All religious people should work for justice in the world.'
Do you agree? Give reasons for your opinion, showing that you have considered another point of view. In your answer, you should refer to at least one religion.

Factfile 37 The nature of punishment

1 Write out a definition of three theories of punishment.

2 Have a class discussion on which theory of punishment is most likely to reduce crime.

Factfile 38 Christianity and punishment

1 Explain why some Christians do not agree with retribution as a form of punishment.

2 Explain why some Christians agree with retribution.

Factfiles 39, 40, 41 Islam, Judaism and Hinduism and punishment

1 Choose one religion other than Christianity and give an outline of its teachings on punishment.

2 'Committing a sin is as bad as committing a crime.'
Do you agree? Give reasons for your opinion, showing that you have considered another point of view. In your answer, you should refer to at least one religion.

Factfiles 43 Capital punishment and 44 Christianity and capital punishment

1 Give three arguments in favour of capital punishment.

2 Give three arguments against capital punishment.

3 Explain why many Christians are opposed to capital punishment.

Factfiles 45, 46, 47 Islam, Judaism and Hinduism and capital punishment

1 Choose one religion other than Christianity and give an outline of its teachings on capital punishment.

2 Have a class discussion on whether capital punishment is an effective form of punishment.

3 'No religious person can agree with capital punishment.'
Do you agree? Give reasons for your opinion, showing that you have considered another point of view. In your answer, you should refer to at least one religion.

MEDICAL TREATMENTS FOR INFERTILITY

Infertility has become much more of a problem in the western world in recent years with as many as ten per cent of couples in the UK estimated to have fertility problems.

Medical technology has provided many solutions which are known as **embryo technology**:

IN-VITRO FERTILISATION (IVF) – WHEN AN EGG FROM THE WOMAN IS FERTILISED OUTSIDE THE WOMB USING EITHER THE HUSBAND'S OR A DONOR'S SPERM AND THEN REPLACED IN THE WOMB.

ARTIFICIAL INSEMINATION BY HUSBAND (AIH) – WHEN THE HUSBAND'S SPERM IS INSERTED INTO HIS WIFE BY MECHANICAL MEANS.

ARTIFICIAL INSEMINATION BY DONOR (AID) – WHEN AN ANONYMOUS MAN DONATES SPERM WHICH IS INSERTED MECHANICALLY INTO THE MOTHER.

EGG DONATION – WHEN AN EGG IS DONATED BY ANOTHER WOMAN AND FERTILISED BY IVF USING THE HUSBAND'S SPERM AND THEN PLACED IN THE WIFE'S WOMB.

EMBRYO DONATION – WHEN BOTH EGG AND SPERM COME FROM DONORS AND ARE FERTILISED USING IVF.

SURROGACY – EITHER WHEN THE EGG AND SPERM OF WIFE AND HUSBAND ARE FERTILISED BY IVF AND THEN PLACED INTO ANOTHER WOMAN'S WOMB; OR WHEN ANOTHER WOMAN IS ARTIFICIALLY INSEMINATED BY THE HUSBAND'S SPERM. IN BOTH CASES, AFTER THE BIRTH THE WOMAN HANDS THE BABY TO THE HUSBAND AND WIFE.

All of these are now being used by couples in Britain supervised by the Human Fertilisation and Embryology Authority, though there have been many arguments about their morality.

This is clearly an issue for religion as many of the opponents of fertility treatments have accused doctors of playing God. However, to the parents concerned, fertility treatments have been regarded as a miracle.

Sarah and Peter's triplets were conceived by IVF.

CHILDREN MAY GET RIGHT TO FIND DONOR PARENTS

Newspaper headline from 20 October 1998 when the Government ordered an investigation into sperm and egg donation which is now running at 2000 births a year.

Sarah and Peter have triplets who were conceived by IVF treatment after years of trying to have children.

When Sarah was asked how she and Peter felt when told they were unlikely to have children, she replied, 'As a woman I felt a failure and excluded. I had a sense that there was this special person who I desperately wanted to meet, but wasn't being allowed to. As a wife, I felt I was a dud.'

Peter, despite genuinely wanting children, was able to be more philosophical. He said, 'As a couple, we felt we were ready to move on to the next stage of our lives, but were suspended in childlessness. We felt real sadness.'

When asked how they felt when offered fertility treatment, Sarah said, 'We never felt it was wrong. We never thought it was tampering with the course of nature or against the will of God. We simply felt that I had a medical condition which was in no way my fault and which needed treatment. We were delighted and optimistic when first offered treatment. The period of treatment was a real emotional rollercoaster. As the years dragged on and we entered the realms of high-tech treatment, I became very worried that it wouldn't work.'

As far as life being parents is concerned, Sarah said, 'Life as parents is exhausting and hard work, but excellent. We feel a sense of the future and continuation. The babies give us a lot of happiness and laughter, which outweighs all the worry and loss of our relatively hedonistic lifestyle. They are a real gift to us.'

CHRISTIANITY AND INFERTILITY

Techniques that entail the disassociation of husband and wife, by the intrusion of a person other than the couple... are gravely immoral. These techniques infringe the child's right to be born of a father and mother known to him and bound to each other by marriage ... Techniques involving only the married couple ... are perhaps less reprehensible yet remain morally unacceptable. They dissociate the sexual act from the procreative act.

Catechism of the Catholic Church

The Division of the Methodist Church responsible for advising the Church on medical ethics has accepted for the time being the scientific judgement that remedies for human infertility, and for certain genetic diseases and handicaps, would be greatly assisted if research on embryos not required for artificial insemination continues to be carried out ... that investigation ... is permissible up to fourteen days.

Statement of the Methodist Church in What the Churches Say.

Adoption can give a couple children and then grandchildren.

There are two very different Christian views on infertility.

1 The Roman Catholic view is that life is given by God and that no one has a right to children. Although the Catholic Church feels great sympathy for the childless who want children, it only allows methods which do not threaten the sacredness of life and in which sex acts are natural. This means that all embryo technology is banned for Catholics. The reasons for this attitude are:

- IVF involves fertilising several eggs some of which are thrown away or used for experimentation which is the same as abortion;

- all forms of artificial insemination or surrogacy involve masturbation by the male which is a sin for Catholics;

- Catholics believe children have the right to know who their parents are and this is prevented in AID and surrogacy;

- all forms of embryo technology involve fertilisation taking place apart from the sex act. Catholics believe that God intended procreation to be a part of the sex act.

2 The other Christian Churches allow IVF and AIH because:

- it is good to use technology to provide couples with the joy of children;

- the egg and sperm are from the husband and wife;

- the discarded embryos are not foetuses and their destruction can be justified by the doctrine of double effect (the intention is to produce children for childless couples not to kill embryos).

They have major concerns about all other embryo technology, though none have actually been banned by the Churches. They feel that all the other methods involve questions of who the parent is and could lead to problems for the children in terms of their identity and also legal issues about exactly who the parents are.

All Christians would encourage childless couples to adopt.

Most Muslims accept IVF and AIH when couples are having fertility problems because:

- these are simply using medicine to bring about the family life which all Muslims are expected to have;

- the egg and sperm are from the husband and wife;

- the discarded embryos are not foetuses and their destruction can be justified by the doctrine of double effect (the intention is to produce children for childless couples not to kill embryos).

However, Islamic lawyers have banned all the other types of embryo technology because they deny a child's right to know its natural parents and they are very similar to adoption which is banned in Islam.

If the semen of a man is placed in an artificial womb ... the action is permissible and ... all orders applicable to a father and child will be applicable to them... Making the semen of a husband reach the womb of his wife artificially is permissible and the child thus born is like all other children.

Articles of Islamic Acts, Imam Al-Khoei.

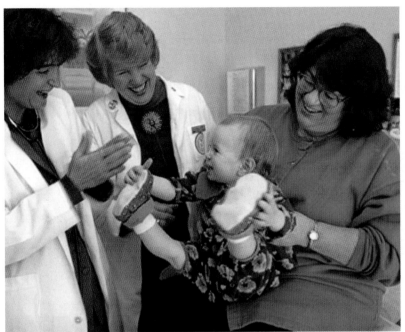

Is it really wrong to conceive children by AID, as this child was?

In Islam, family life is governed by laws taken directly from the Qur'an and the Sunnah ... hence there are areas and topics where changes in those laws cannot even be contemplated ... No Muslim man is allowed to donate sperm to a woman who is not his legal wife and no woman is allowed to donate an egg to another woman. No child can be called after a person unless the sperm is that of the person to whom he belongs and he has been borne (and born) by the woman who is the legal wife of the man concerned ... If a married woman conceives using sperm from a third party because her husband is infertile, this is adultery ... If a woman carries an embryo fertilised with the sperm and egg of another couple, the child legally belongs to the 'surrogate mother'.

Statement from the Islamic Shari'ah Council of Britain published in *What Does Islam Say*, Ibrahim Hewitt.

JUDAISM AND INFERTILITY

One day Elisha went to Shunem. And a well-to-do woman was there, who urged him to stay for a meal. So whenever he came by, he stopped there to eat ... 'What can be done for her?' Elisha asked. Gehazi said, 'Well, she has no son and her husband is old.'
Then Elisha said, 'Call her.' So he called her, and she stood in the doorway ... 'About this time next year,' Elisha said, 'you will hold a son in your arms.'

2 Kings 4:8–15

IVF and AIH are accepted by all Jews and many accept egg donation. Some feel that the egg must be donated by a Jewish woman to make the baby Jewish, but others think that upbringing is enough. Jews believe this because:

- having children is extremely important in the Jewish faith and for the preservation of Judaism;

- rabbis are very supportive to couples who are having fertility problems;

- God intends humans to use the benefits of technology as long as it is within the mitzvot;

- the discarded embryos are not foetuses and their destruction can be justified by the doctrine of double effect (the intention is to produce children for childless couples not to kill embryos).

However, most Jews would not allow AID as it is seen as a form of adultery and so is not allowed, and children have the right to know who their natural parents are. Surrogacy is not allowed as it is felt that whoever gives birth to a child is the mother and Jewishness is passed on by the mother.

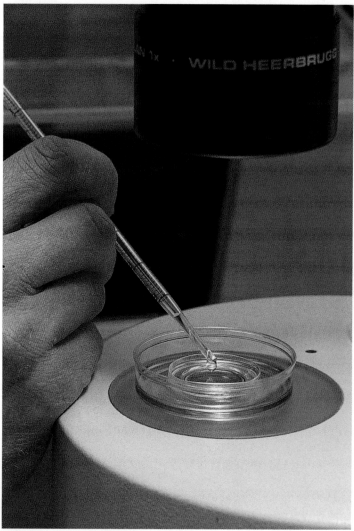

Life for some children now begins in a glass dish.

Most Hindu couples long for children, especially a son. The Law of Manu encourages infertile couples to adopt from a relative which works well in India where there are large families. However, few Hindu families in Britain would be prepared to do this and so Hindu couples are turning to embryo technology. Hinduism has no problems with IVF and AIH because:

- these are simply using medicine to bring about the family life which all Hindus are expected to have;

- the egg and sperm are from the husband and wife;

- the discarded embryos are not foetuses, no soul has been transferred to them.

However, AID and embryo donation are not allowed. Hindus believe this because caste is passed down through the father. Most Hindus disapprove of egg donation and surrogacy, but some would allow it if there are strict safeguards and all other methods have been tried.

HINDUISM AND INFERTILITY

The one who rules over both knowledge and ignorance ... alone presides over womb after womb, and thus over all visible forms and all the sources of birth.

Svetasvatara Upanishad 5:1–2

Should couples be allowed to adopt children over the Internet?

GENETIC ENGINEERING

Genetic engineering is 'the deliberate modification of the characters of an organism by the manipulation of the genetic material' (*OED*). In connection with medical issues (which is all you have to study) it is using techniques of gene development and manipulation to find cures or prevention for disease and disabilities in humans.

Genetic diseases affect large numbers of people. Defective inherited genes can cause mental retardation, physical deformity or early death. Scientists are involved in genetic research into: cystic fybrosis, muscular dystrophy, sickle-cell anaemia, Tay-Sachs disease and Huntington's chorea. They have been helped by the Human Genome Project which is mapping all the genes in the human body.

Most genetic research has been based on germline gene therapy to enable genetic changes to be made to those cells that transmit information from one generation to the next enabling permanent changes to be made. However, more recently cloning processes have been used to grow healthy cells to replace the malfunctioning ones and so cure disease. This process involves creating stem cells either from embryos produced for IVF but not used, or from adult bone marrow or blood. These stem cells are then cultivated and kept alive so that they can multiply and be transplanted into diseased cells to produce a cure.

DISABLED MPs PLEAD FOR CELL STEM RESEARCH

'Arrogant to deny sufferers of chronic diseases the chance of a cure,' says Labour MP. Addressing the House from her wheelchair, Anne Begg appealed to MPs with strong religious convictions not to deny those suffering from devastating illnesses the chance of a cure.

Newspaper report 16 December 2000.

Stem cell researchers hope to produce cures for fatal diseases.

In the United Kingdom, stem cell research was illegal because the Human Fertilisation and Embryology Act 1990 said that such research could only be used for the treatment of infertility. However, legislation permitting the research was passed by Parliament in February 2001.

Non-religious arguments in favour of genetic engineering

- It offers the prospect of cures for currently incurable diseases.

- It is being done in other countries and so is available to those rich enough to travel and pay for treatments.

- Research into stem cell cloning would only use embryos until it was easier to use adult cells.

- Genetic research is an integral part of medical research and is bound to include some genetic engineering.

- Genetic research is closely monitored by the law, but has vast potential benefits.

Non-religious arguments against genetic engineering

Genetic engineering:

- has too little information about the long-term consequences;

- has effects which would be irreversible, so if anything went wrong it would be permanent;

- places too much power in the hands of scientists who could use genetic engineering to act like Dr Frankenstein to produce scientifically created human beings;

- treats the human body as a commodity no different from plants;

- offers the possibility of people having to be genetically screened before getting life insurance, senior jobs etc with anyone likely to develop illness or die young being refused.

CHRISTIANITY AND GENETIC ENGINEERING

There are several attitudes to genetic engineering amongst Christians.

Some Christians, **mainly liberal Protestants**, believe that genetic engineering is a good thing which should be supported by the Church as long as it is done for the cure of disease and not to produce 'perfect humans'. Such Christians support the work of the Human Fertilisation and Embryology Authority which supervises genetic engineering using human embryos. They support genetic engineering because:

- Jesus was a healer who showed that Christians should do all they can to cure disease;

- discovering the genetic make-up of humans and using those discoveries to improve human life is part of what God wants humans to do as stewards of his creation. It is no different from researching into drugs which can be used to improve human life;

- there is a difference between creating cells and creating people. Creating people by science rather than sex would be wrong because it would be taking over God's role in the creation of life, but creating cells is working with God;

- as far as using embryos for genetic research is concerned, embryos cannot be regarded as potential human life until they are 14 days old (the time limit set by the Human Fertilisation and Embryology Authority for genetic research);

- they accept most of the non-religious arguments in favour of genetic engineering.

Some Christians, **mainly Roman Catholics**, believe that genetic engineering is permissible as long as it is only for curing diseases and does not use human embryos. They agree with genetic research for the same first three reasons as liberal Protestants, but disagree with the use of embryos because:

- life begins at the moment of conception whether in a womb or a glass dish;

- killing an embryo is killing human life which is banned by the Bible and the Church;

- embryos for research have been produced by methods with which the Catholic Church disagrees (see Factfile 49).

Some Christians are opposed to any form of genetic research at all. They have this attitude because:

- they believe that God has created the genetic make-up of each human being at the moment of conception and people have no right to interfere with God's will;

- they believe that genetic engineering is 'playing God', and that is a great sin;

- they believe that it is wrong to try to make the earth perfect, as only heaven is perfect. This life is a preparation for heaven and should not be used to try to make heaven on earth;

- they accept the non-religious arguments against genetic engineering.

Should Christian leaders like the Archbishop of Westminster try to influence politicians in their decisions on genetic engineering?

We write to you as leaders of the Catholic community in Great Britain to express our deep concern over the issue of human cloning. The Government's decision to press ahead with proposals to allow so-called therapeutic cloning is deeply worrying, not only to our own communities, but also to many peoples of all faiths and none.

While the end – research into treatments for disease using stem cells – is good in itself, the means being proposed are quite immoral. To create and destroy human lives simply to extract cells for research is wrong. Such procedures use human lives as disposable objects.

From a letter to *The Times* from the Roman Catholic Archbishops of Westminster and Glasgow, 14 December 2000

Jesus of Nazareth was a healer. He cured diseases, and showed that God's purposes include overcoming 'those things in His creation that spoil it and that diminish the life of his children.' Clearly, where genetic manipulation is the means of healing diseases – in animals or humans – it is to be welcomed.

Statement from the Methodist Church in *What the Churches Say*.

When you enter a town and are welcomed, eat what is set before you. Heal the sick who are there and tell them, 'The kingdom of God is near you.'

Luke 10:8–9

ISLAM AND GENETIC ENGINEERING

Some Muslims are opposed to genetic research in any form at all. They have this attitude because:

- they believe that the genetic make-up of each individual person has been established by God and only God can alter that make-up;

- they believe that embryo research is the same as abortion, and, as they believe life begins at fertilisation and do not agree with abortion, they will not allow genetic research;

- they believe that scientists who are trying to create life from stem cells etc are acting as God and this is the unforgivable sin for a Muslim (shirk);

- they accept many of the non-religious arguments against genetic engineering.

Some Muslims believe that genetic engineering is a good thing as long as it is done for the cure of disease and not to produce 'perfect humans'. Such Muslims support the work of the Human Fertilisation and Embryology Authority which supervises genetic engineering using human embryos. They support genetic engineering because:

- the Qur'an and hadith teach that Muslims should do all they can to cure disease;

- discovering the genetic make-up of humans and using those discoveries to improve human life is part of what God wants humans to do as vice-gerents of his creation. It is no different from researching into drugs which can be used to improve human life;

- there is a difference between creating cells and creating people. Creating people by science rather than sex would be wrong because it would be taking over God's role in the creation of life, but creating cells is working with God;

- as far as using embryos for genetic research is concerned, embryos cannot be regarded as potential human life until they are 14 days old (the time limit set by the Human Fertilisation and Embryology Authority for genetic research which fits in with the teachings of the Shari'ah on abortion).

The human genome project may give scientists all the information they need to create life.

Some Jews, **mainly Orthodox**, believe that genetic engineering is permissible as long as it is only for curing diseases and does not use human embryos. They agree with genetic research because:

- the Tenakh and Talmud teach that Jews should do all they can to cure disease;

- discovering the genetic make-up of humans and using those discoveries to improve human life is part of what God wants humans to do as stewards of his creation. It is no different from researching into drugs which can be used to improve human life;

- there is a difference between creating cells and creating people. Creating people by science rather than sex would be wrong because it would be taking over God's role in the creation of life, but creating cells is working with God.

But they disagree with the use of embryos because:

- life begins at the moment of conception whether in a womb or a glass dish;

- killing an embryo is killing human life which is banned by the mitzvot;

- embryos for research have been produced by methods with which Judaism disagrees.

Some Jews agree with genetic engineering, including embryo research, as long as it is done within guidelines set down by the Government to protect society from scientific Frankensteins. They believe this because:

- the Tenakh and Talmud teach that Jews should do all they can to cure disease;

- discovering the genetic make-up of humans and using those discoveries to improve human life is part of what God wants humans to do as stewards of his creation. It is no different from researching into drugs which can be used to improve human life;

- there is a difference between creating cells and creating people. Creating people by science rather than sex would be wrong because it would be taking over God's role in the creation of life, but creating cells is working with God;

- as far as using embryos for genetic research is concerned, embryos cannot be regarded as potential human life until they are 14 days old (the time limit set by the Human Fertilisation and Embryology Authority for genetic research).

JUDAISM AND GENETIC ENGINEERING

Whoever destroys a single life is considered as if he had destroyed the whole world, and whoever saves a single life as if he had saved the whole world.

Mishnah

HINDUISM AND GENETIC ENGINEERING

> **When a man rightly sees, he sees no death, no sickness or distress. When a man rightly sees, he sees all.**
>
> *Chandogya Upanishad 7.26.2*

Most Hindus believe genetic engineering is a good thing as long as it is done for the cure of disease and not to produce 'perfect humans'. Such Hindus support the work of the Human Fertilisation and Embryology Authority which supervises genetic engineering using human embryos. They support genetic engineering because:

- Hindus should do all they can to cure disease;

- discovering the genetic make-up of humans and using those discoveries to improve human life is part of the dharma of doctors. It is no different from researching into drugs which can be used to improve human life;

- there is a difference between creating cells and creating people. Creating people by science rather than sex would be wrong because it would be taking over God's role in the creation of life, but creating cells is working with God;

- as far as using embryos for genetic research is concerned, embryos cannot be regarded as potential human life until they are 14 days old (the time limit set by the Human Fertilisation and Embryology Authority).

Muscular dystrophy could be cured by stem cell research using information from the human genome project.

Some Hindus are opposed to any form of genetic engineering. They will not even allow research which does not use embryos. They have this attitude because:

- they believe that genetic research is breaking the law of karma. If a person is intended to suffer from a disease, such as muscular dystrophy, because of their previous bad deeds, they should not try to avoid this by genetic engineering. They will only have to suffer it again in a future life;

- they believe in ahimsa and genetic engineering can be seen as doing violence to the genetic make-up of a person.

Transplant surgery is the use of organs taken from one person and put into another person to replace an organ that is malfunctioning or diseased. A wide range of organs can now be transplanted successfully (from hearts to eye corneas), but there are problems in that the organs have to be compatible, and drugs usually have to be used to prevent the donated organ being rejected by the host. However, transplant surgery is very effective and gives life and hope to people for whom there is otherwise no hope.

There are two types of transplant surgery – one uses organs from a dead person, the other uses organs from a living person which they can live without (e.g. bone-marrow, single kidneys).

Non-religious arguments in favour of transplant surgery

- It is an effective and proven method of curing life-threatening diseases (e.g. heart or kidney malfunction) and improving people's lives (e.g. cornea grafting giving sight to the blind).

- It uses organs which would otherwise be buried or burned.

- It gives people a chance to help others after their death.

- It brings life out of death.

Non-religious arguments against transplant surgery

- It is very expensive and requires high level skills for a very few people.

- It raises the problem of *when* someone is dead as such things as heart transplants require the heart to be removed before it has stopped beating.

- It raises the moral/emotional problem of: will surgeons who have a patient desperate for a transplant work to the best of their ability to save the life of a potential donor?

- It diverts resources from prevention or less expensive cures which could improve the lives of far more people than a transplant.

- It causes a trade in organs from people in the developing world to rich people in the developed world.

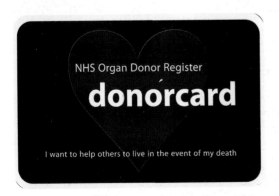

TRANSPLANT SURGERY

JODIE CLINGS TO LIFE AFTER SIAMESE TWINS SEPARATED

The Siamese twins, Jodie and Mary, were separated on 7 November 2000 using the skills of transplant surgery. The twins were joined at the base of their spines, but Mary's heart quickly failed and then her lungs so that she was using her sister as a life support machine. This was putting such a strain on Jodie's organs that doctors thought it likely they would both die within six months. However, the operation to separate the twins would kill Mary whilst saving Jodie's life. The doctors at St Mary's Hospital, Manchester, had to obtain a decision from the Court of Appeal before they could perform the operation against the wishes of the twins' Roman Catholic parents. Mary died during the operation, but Jodie survived and is likely to have a normal life.

CHRISTIANITY AND TRANSPLANT SURGERY

Most Christians agree with transplant surgery, and many Christians carry donor cards so that their organs can be used for others after their death. However, they would object to rich people or surgeons in the developed world paying for organs from the poor. The reasons for this attitude are:

- Christians who believe in the immortality of the soul, believe that the body is not needed after death and therefore its organs can be used to help the living;

- Christians who believe in resurrection believe St Paul's words that the body will be transformed and that the resurrection body will not need the physical organs;

- Jesus told Christians that they should love their neighbours and treat others as they would wish to be treated by them – both of which justify transplants;

- the Bible is full of statements about not exploiting the poor.

Some Christians are opposed to transplant surgery using organs from dead people, but accept transplants using organs donated by living relatives. They would not allow such organs to be paid for. This attitude is based on:

- the Christian belief that organs such as the heart are an intrinsic part of the individual who has been created by God;

- transplanting organs from the dead into the living is usurping the role of God, and humans do not have the right to act as God;

- organs which can be used from the living are not vital and so can be used to obey Jesus' command to love your neighbour;

- organs cannot be paid for because that is exploiting the poor which is banned in the Bible.

Some Christians do not agree with transplants at all and will not carry a donor card. They have this attitude because:

- they believe that transplants can ignore the sanctity of life;

- they believe that transplanting organs is usurping God's role and it is wrong to 'play God';

- they agree with all the non-religious arguments against transplants.

The case of the Siamese twins Mary and Jodie raised major issues for Christians who believe in transplant surgery. The Roman Catholic Church made submissions to the courts to try to get the separation operation banned. It also offered to care for the twins until their death in a Catholic Hospice in Ravenna, Italy. Roman Catholics, and most Evangelical Protestants, argued that the surgeons were going to murder Mary and use some of her organs to save Jodie. As the Archbishop of Westminster said in a submission to the court, 'Medical intervention would be morally impermissible since God has given humankind the gift of life.'

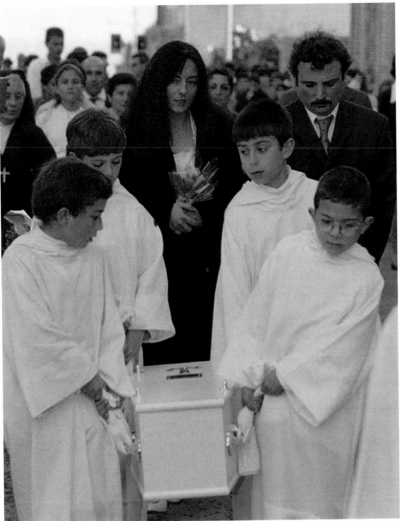

The funeral of Mary, the Siamese twin whose life was sacrificed to save her sister.

However, other Christians supported the operation as Mary was killing Jodie by living off her organs. They felt that the surgeons were acting in defence of Jodie to save her life.

When doctors develop techniques through transplant surgery, then such moral problems are bound to arise. Doctors cannot leave children to die if they have the means to save them.

ISLAM AND TRANSPLANT SURGERY

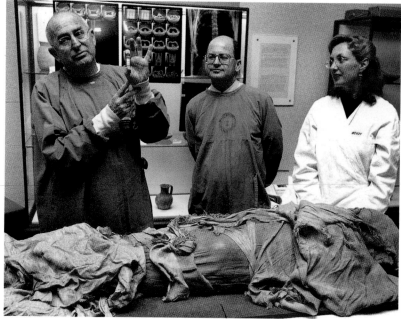

Post-mortems are required by British law when the cause of death is not certain, but they are disapproved of by Islam.

Most Muslims are opposed to transplant surgery and will not carry donor cards. They believe that transplanting organs from one person to another is against God's will. They have this attitude because:

- the Shari'ah teaches that nothing should be removed from the body after death and opposes post-mortems. Therefore organs should not be removed from dead Muslims;

- the Qur'an says that God has created the body of a person and so to take parts from one body and put them into another is to act as God which is the greatest sin of Islam, shirk;

- the Muslim belief in the sanctity of life means that all life belongs to God and only God has the right to give and take life;

- they would also agree with the non-religious arguments against transplants.

Some Muslims allow transplant surgery using organs from a living donor as long as the donor is a close relative. They have this attitude because:

- some Muslim lawyers have said that it is permissible;

- a ruling, fatwa, was issued by the Muslim Law Council of the United Kingdom in 1995 saying that Muslims could carry donor cards and have transplants;

- Islam aims to do good and is not intended to put burdens on people which they cannot bear. If a close relative is dying and a transplant would save them, then it should be given, just as pork can be eaten if a Muslim would otherwise starve to death;

- they would also agree with the non-religious arguments in favour of transplants.

Most Jews allow transplant surgery using organs from a living donor as long as the donor is a close relative. They have this attitude because:

- Jews believe that organs such as the heart are an intrinsic part of the individual who has been created by God;

- organs from non-Jews might affect one's Jewishness (being a Jew is passed on by the blood of the mother);

- transplanting organs from the dead into the living is usurping the role of God, and humans do not have the right to act as God;

- organs which can be used from the living are not vital and so can be used to obey the mitzvah to preserve life;

- organs cannot be paid for because that is exploiting the poor which is banned in the Torah and Tenakh.

Some Jews are opposed to transplant surgery and will not carry donor cards. They believe that transplanting organs from one person to another is against God's will. They have this attitude because:

- they believe that transplanting organs is breaking the mitzvot on the sanctity of life;

- they believe that the organs have been created by God for a specific individual and cannot be put into someone else. They are particularly concerned that transplants may affect people's Jewishness;

- they would also agree with all the non-religious arguments against transplants.

JUDAISM AND TRANSPLANT SURGERY

Heart transplants keep people alive through someone else's death.

HINDUISM AND TRANSPLANT SURGERY

Most Hindus allow transplant surgery and would carry donor cards. They have this attitude because:

- they believe that the body is not important, it is the soul which matters. When someone dies, it is their body which dies, their soul will be reborn into another body. As the dead body will be burned, its organs can be used to help others;

- as the soul is the immortal part of a person, it does not matter which bits are added to or taken away from the body;

- they would also agree with the non-religious arguments in favour of transplant surgery.

Some Hindus are opposed to any form of transplant surgery and will not carry donor cards. They have this attitude because:

- they believe that transplants are trying to break the law of karma. If a person is intended to suffer from a bad heart because of their previous bad deeds, they should not try to avoid this by having a transplant;

- they believe in ahimsa and transplant surgery is doing violence to the person from whom the organ is taken;

- they are worried that poor people may be tempted to sell their organs, or even die to provide money for their family.

QUESTIONS

Factfile 48 Medical treatments for infertility

1   Make a list of the treatments available for infertility.

2   Have a class discussion on which treatments should be available and whether any should not.

Factfile 49 Christianity and infertility

1   Give an outline of the Roman Catholic attitude to fertility treatments.

2   Give an account of the Protestant attitude to infertility treatments.

Factfiles 50, 51, 52 Islam, Judaism and Hinduism and infertility

1   Choose one religion other than Christianity and give an account of its teachings on infertility treatments.

2   'If God wants people to have children, they will have them without using fertility treatments.'
Do you agree? Give reasons for your opinion, showing that you have considered another point of view. In your answer, you should refer to at least one religion.

Factfile 53 Genetic engineering

1   What is meant by genetic engineering?

2   Give three non-religious arguments against genetic engineering.

3   Give three non-religious arguments in favour of genetic engineering.

Factfile 54 Christianity and genetic engineering

1   Explain why some Christians are opposed to genetic engineering.

2   Explain why some Christians are in favour of genetic engineering.

Factfiles 55, 56, 57 Islam, Judaism and Hinduism and genetic engineeering

1   Choose one religion other than Christianity and give an outline of its attitudes to genetic engineering.

2   'Only God should interfere with our genes.'
Do you agree? Give reasons for your opinion, showing that you have considered another point of view. In your answer, you should refer to at least one religion.

Factfile 58 Transplant surgery

1   Give an outline of the different types of transplant surgery.

2   Have a class discussion on the morality of transplant surgery.

Factfile 59 Christianity and genetic engineering

1   Give an outline of Christian attitudes to transplant surgery.

2   Explain why Christians have different attitudes to transplant surgery.

Factfiles 60, 61, 62 Islam, Judaism and Hinduism and genetic engineeeing

1   Choose one religion other than Christianity and give an outline of its attitudes to transplant surgery.

2   'No religious person can have a heart transplant.'
Do you agree? Give reasons for your opinion, showing that you have considered another point of view. In your answer, you should refer to at least one religion.

6 RELIGION AND SCIENCE

THE BIBLICAL COSMOLOGY

Cosmology is the word given to the study of the origin and structure of the universe.

There are two accounts of creation in the Bible.

According to Genesis chapter 1, God created the whole universe in six days in the following way:

Day 1   heaven and earth, light and dark

Day 2   the separation of the earth from the sky

Day 3   the dry land, plants and trees

Day 4   the sun, moon and stars

Day 5   fish and birds

Day 6   animals and humans.

Each part of the creation came about because of God's words: 'God said, "Let there be light," and there was light' (Genesis 1:3).

Humans were made at the same time and were made in the image of God: 'So God created man in his own image; in the image of God he created him; male and female he created them.' (Genesis 1:27). Humans were also made to have authority over the world: 'Let us make man in our image, in our likeness, and let them rule over the fish of the sea and the birds of the air, over the livestock, over all the earth' (Genesis 1:26).

When God had finished the creation, it was perfect: 'God saw all that he had made and it was very good' (Genesis 1:31).

According to Genesis chapter 2, God created things in the following way:

1 God created the heavens and the earth.

2 God formed man from the dust of the earth and breathed life into him.

3 God made trees grow out of the ground and formed the Garden of Eden.

4 God placed Adam in the Garden of Eden.

5 God thought Adam would be lonely, so he created birds and animals which Adam named.

6 The birds and animals were not suitable helpers for Adam, so God put Adam to sleep, removed one of his ribs, and from the rib he created woman, Eve.

Adam and Eve in the Garden of Eden by Dora Holzhandler
(1993).

Most Christians see Genesis chapter 2 as a commentary on
chapter 1 rather than a different story, especially as Genesis
chapter 2 carries on into chapter 3 which explains how Adam
and Eve sinned and were thrown out of the Garden so that evil
and suffering came into the world.

THE ISLAMIC COSMOLOGY

There is no single story of creation in Islam such as the stories in Genesis, though there are many references to creation. As a result of this, two Islamic cosmologies have arisen:

1 The traditional view

This argues from surah 7:54 that God created the earth, the heavens and life in six days – 'Your Guardian-Lord is God, who created the heavens and the earth in six days.'

Although there are no clear statements about the order of creation, there are statements in the Qur'an which state that God:

- created the sun, moon, stars and planets (7:54);

- separated night from day (7:54);

- sent water to the earth and created vegetation (20:53);

- created birds, fish and animals (16:5–8);

- created Adam as the first human being, Adam was made out of clay into which God breathed life (23:12–16);

- created Adam as the khalifah of the earth and made the angels bow to Adam because Adam had been given free will (2:30–34);

- threw Adam and his wife out of the Garden for giving in to the temptation of Satan (2:35–36);

- creates by speaking (2:117).

This gives the idea of God creating everything directly in six days and that all humans have descended from God's direct creation Adam and his wife.

2 The modern view

This is argued clearly in *The Qur'an and Modern Science* by M Bucaille.

- It claims that the Arabic word translated as days in English is more correctly translated as 'ages'. So the Islamic view is that God's creation took six ages.

- There is no sequence of creation in the Qur'an, but the first creation appears to be the heavens and indeed there is reference to their motion: 'All the celestial bodies swim around, each in its rounded course' (21:33).

- Then God created life from the water: 'We made from water every living thing' (21:30).

- From this came vegetation: 'Sent down water from the sky with it have we produced divers pairs of plants' (20:53).

- God created man from an embryo formed from semen (22:5).

This gives the idea of a gradual creation with a more evolutionary character.

Front cover of Qur'an and Modern Science.

As the Book of Genesis is regarded as the word of God by both Christians and Jews, the Jewish cosmology is exactly the same as the Christian one. You should use the Christian cosmology in Factfile 63 to answer questions on the Jewish cosmology.

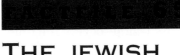

THE JEWISH COSMOLOGY

THE HINDU COSMOLOGY

As Hinduism has so many varieties, there are many different stories of creation. However, there are two main types of cosmology in Hinduism.

1 The cosmology based on myths

This view of cosmology is based on stories in the Vedas. A typical one is the Primal man Myth from Rig Veda X 90.

Purusha (Primal Man) fills the universe and the visible world is only a quarter of his greatness.

Purusha sacrificed himself and from his sacrifice came the universe and all that is in it, especially the Vedas and the castes of humans. The sun comes from his eye, the earth from his feet, the great gods Indra and Agni from his mouth. Also from his mouth came the Brahmins, from his arms the Kshatriya (warriors/nobles), from his thighs the Vaishya (farmers, traders, artisans), from his feet the Shudras (labourers).

Many Hindus believe the universe is in continual creation.

2 The cosmology based on ideas

This view is based on the philosophical ideas contained in writings such as the Upanishads.

Typical is the Chandogya Upanishad which claims that there is a universal force behind the universe, Brahman, which sends out, sustains and then re-absorbs the universe in an unending series. Therefore the creation of the universe is just like samsara. The universe is born, it lives, it dies, it is reborn. What stays for ever is Brahman and the soul.

As a result of scientific discoveries over the past two hundred years, most scientists now accept a cosmology which is based on science rather than religion.

Discoveries in physics have shown that matter is eternal, it can neither be created nor destroyed, it can only be changed.

Scientists believe that the universe began about 15 billion years ago with a Big Bang when the matter of the universe became so compressed that it produced a huge explosion (evidence for this can be seen in the Red Shift effect when looking at distant galaxies).

As the matter flew away from the explosion, the forces of gravity etc. joined some together into stars and about five billion years ago the solar system formed.

CHAPTER 16

THE SCIENTIFIC COSMOLOGY

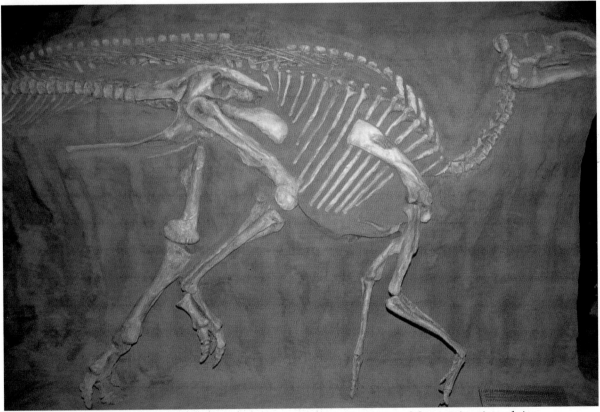

Many scientists claim dinosaurs are evidence for the scientific cosmology.

Primitive life began on earth 4.5 billion years ago and developed through evolution. Evolution is the name given to the theory that life on earth began as very primitive basic life forms such as amoeba and developed through the process of natural selection (in every generation there are mutations and if there is a mutation which is better adapted to its environment, this mutation will reproduce and become a new species) to animal and plant life. It also claims that humans evolved from animals so that about 2.5 million years ago, humans first appeared.

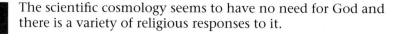

The scientific cosmology seems to have no need for God and there is a variety of religious responses to it.

RELIGIOUS ATTITUDES TO THE SCIENTIFIC COSMOLOGY

Christian responses

Many Christians simply ignore the scientific cosmology, but of those who think about it, there are the following responses:

1 Creationism
This view says that science is wrong and the Bible is right. It claims that all the evidence there is of the Big Bang and evolution can be explained by the effects of Noah's flood (which must have totally changed rock formations) and the Apparent Age Theory.

Apparent Age Theory claims that if you accept the Bible view, then when Adam was made the earth was six days old, but to Adam it would have looked billions of years old because trees would have been created with rings showing them hundreds of years old; the Grand Canyon would have looked two billion years old when it was one second old.

2 Conservatism

This view says that both science and the Bible are correct. The main points of the Bible story fit with science. One of God's days could be millions or billions of years. They claim that Genesis 1:3 'God said, "Let there be light"', is a direct reference to the Big Bang and that the order of creation in plants, trees, fish, birds, animals, humans is the order of science.

A spiral galaxy forming in the aftermath of the Big Bang.

3 Liberalism

This view says that the Bible is not meant to be regarded as true, it is a story told to give the vital piece of truth that God created everything. Many liberal Christians and Jews are scientists who claim that the scientific cosmology is so remarkable that it means it was the way God used to create humans.

They claim this because:

- the Big Bang had to be at exactly the right micro second. If it had been too soon it would have been too small to form stars, if it had been too late, everything would have flown away too fast for stars to form;

- the way stars are formed out of hydrogen and helium and by nucleic reactions produce carbon and oxygen which are spread around the universe by exploding supernovae implies a creator organising things;

- the way in which life on earth requires carbon to be able to bond with four other atoms and water molecules could not have happened by chance.

So they feel that Big Bang and evolution could only have happened if God made them happen and they claim that even at the moment of the Big Bang, the nature of matter and the laws of science mean that humans were bound to appear.

> **Your guardian Lord is God who created the heavens and the earth in six days and is firmly established on the throne of authority.**
>
> *Surah 7:54*

> **God saw all that he had made, and it was very good. And there was evening and there was morning – the sixth day.**
>
> *Genesis 1:31*

> **Matter evolves into material form by virtue of its own potentialities and requires no other agency to effect the transformation.**
>
> *Vishnu Purana 1.4.52*

> The notion to be derived from the Qur'an is one of a con-comitance in the celestial and terrestrial evolutions. There is also fundamental data concerning the existence of intial gaseous mass (dukhan) which is unique and whose elements, although at first fused together (ratq), subsequently became separated (fatq).
>
> *The Qur'an and Modern Science*, M. Bucaille.

> The Big Bang theory implies the act of a God who intended to create beings like us.
>
> *A Brief History of Time*, Stephen Hawking

Muslim responses

Muslims who believe in the traditional cosmology tend to ignore the scientific cosmology.

Those who believe in the modern cosmology find no difficulties with the scientific cosmology as they believe it is referred to in the Qur'an. They believe that God created the matter of the universe, the Big Bang and the laws of science which led to the formation of stars, planets, life and evolution, though they usually believe that God intervened to create humans by breathing souls into them to make humans different from the rest of creation.

Jewish responses

Jewish responses are similar to Christian ones, though few Jews would use the creationist arguments. Most Jews would agree with either the conservative or liberal view.

Hindu responses

Most Hindus who believe in the mythical cosmology would not think about the scientific cosmology.

Hindus who believe in the cosmology based on ideas, feel that the scientific cosmology is proof of their view. They believe that the Big Bang was just the start of this phase of creation and that eventually the universe will contract and then explode again to create a new universe and this will go on for ever.

> What is revealed of the divine in the human life of Jesus is also to be discerned in the cosmic story of creation.
>
> *Science and Creation*, J. Polkinghorne

> The point is that, for the existence of any forms of life that we may conceive, the necessary environment, whatever its nature, must be complex and dependent on a multiplicity of coincident conditions, such as are not reasonably attributable to blind forces or to pure mechanism.
>
> F R Tennant quoted in *The Existence of God*, ed. J. Hick.

Many people think that science and religion are totally different from each other. They think that science is about facts, but religion is about unprovable things which cannot happen. Because of these ideas, they think that scientists have nothing to do with religion. However, this is not true. There are scientists who have been led to believe in God through science and many religious people think that science and religion are two ways of looking at the same facts.

HOW SCIENCE AND RELIGION ARE CONNECTED

1 Christianity, Islam, Judaism, Hinduism, Buddhism and Sikhism all claim that the universe has been made by God in some way, and that if the universe is investigated it will be seen that there are laws of nature which show that God has designed everything.

In the same way, science claims that the universe works on laws or principles which work whether humans know them or not. Science is based on everything having an explanation and religion says that God is the explanation.

2 Science says that objects in the world can be affected by forces which cannot be detected by human senses e.g. gravity, magnetism. Science says that these unseen forces can only be observed by their effects.

The heavens declare the glory of God; the skies proclaim the work of his hands.

Psalm 19:1

In the same way, religion claims that human beings can be affected by a force which cannot be detected by human senses, a force they call God. This unseen force, God, can only be observed through its effects on human lives.

3 Science and religion often use the same methods.

Scientists see things happening in the world, then work out a theory to explain why they are happening and then test out that theory by experiment e.g. observing that a candle goes out if it is covered, work out a theory that burning requires air, then carry out experiments removing the air when things are burning to see whether things can burn without air.

In the same way if someone claims to be a prophet sent from God, religious experts would test the claim by experiment: how does the prophet's teaching and lifestyle compare with previous prophets, does the prophet affect people's lives by making them better people, does the prophet bring people to God.

The beauty and order of the solar system lead many astronomers to believe in God.

> **Behold! In the creation of the heavens and the earth; in the alternation of the night and the day ... In the rain which God sends down from the skies and the life which he gives therewith to an earth which is dead; in the beasts of all kinds ... here indeed are signs for a people that is wise.'**
>
> *Surah 2:164*

4 Most religions would say that a study of science leads to an awareness of God and many scientists are deeply religious because their science has brought them into contact with God. They look at the order and design in such things as DNA and think it is too complicated and beautiful to be an accident. Many mathematicians think that the whole universe works on mathematical principles which they discover through research. If the principles are there waiting to be discovered, they must have been put there by God.

Other religious scientists say that science is based on everything having an explanation and so the universe must have an explanation and the only explanation of why the universe is here is God.

5 Although science is more easy to prove than religion, both science and religion rely on belief and experience. A scientist believes that things do not happen by chance and that everything has an explanation and then tests that belief by their experience of science. A religious person believes in God and then tests that belief by their experience of life.

> Nature is as divine a text as the Holy Scriptures. They can't be in real contradiction of each other.

Galileo

Einstein.

> Science without religion is handicapped: Religion without science is blind.

Einstein

QUESTIONS

Factfile 63 The biblical cosmology

1 Give a definition of cosmology.

2 Give an outline of the biblical cosmology.

Factfiles 64, 65, 66 The Islamic, Jewish and Hindu cosmology

Choose one religion other than Christianity and give an outline of the traditional cosmology of that religion.

Factfile 67 The scientific cosmology

1 Give an outline of the scientific cosmology.

2 Explain why some people think the scientific cosmology disproves religion.

Factfile 68 Religious attitudes to the scientific cosmology

1 Explain how some Christians connect the scientific and Christian cosmologies.

2 Explain why some Christians reject the scientific cosmology.

3 Choose one religion other than Christianity and explain how its followers connect the scientific and religious cosmologies.

4 'God made the world.'
Do you agree? Give reasons for your opinion, showing that you have considered another point of view. In your answer, you should refer to at least one religion.

Factfile 69 How religion and science are connected

1 Give an outline of the similarities between what science and religion think about the nature of the universe.

2 State what is similar about the way religion and science test things.

3 Explain why some scientists believe in God.

4 'Science has disproved religion.'
Do you agree? Give reasons for your opinion, showing that you have considered another point of view. In your answer, you should refer to at least one religion.

Useful addresses

Amnesty International
99–119 Roseberry Avenue
London EC1R 4RE

Animals in Medicine Research Information Centre
12 Whitehall
London SW1A 2DY

BBC Religious Broadcasting
New Broadcasting House
Oxford Road
Manchester M60 1SJ

Board of Deputies of British Jews
Woburn House
Upper Woburn Place
London WC1H 0EP

The Bourne Trust (Christian group helping prisoners and their families)
Lincoln House
1 Brixton Road
London SW9 6DE

CAFOD
2 Romero Close
Stockwell Road
London SW9 9TY

Catholic Truth Society
38–40 Eccleston Square
London SW1V 1PD

Channel 4 TV
60 Charlotte Street
London W1P 2AX

The Children's Society
Edward Rudolf House
Margery Street
London W1X 0JL

Christian Aid
PO Box 100
London SW1 7RT

Christian Animal Rights Education
PO Box 407
Sheffield S1 1ED

Christian Communication Bureau
4 Hindes Road
Harrow
Middlesex HA1 1SJ

Christian Ecology Group
c/o Mrs Joan Hart
17 Burns Gardens
Lincoln LN2 4LJ

Christian Education Movement
Royal Buildings
Victoria Street
Derby DE1 1GW

Church of England Information Office
Church House
Dean's Yard
London SW1P 3NZ

ISKCON (International Society for Krishna Consciousness)
10 Soho Street
London W1V 5FA

Islamic Foundation
Markfield Dawah Centre
Ratby Lane
Markfield
Leicester LE67 9RN

Islamic Relief
19 Rea Street South
Birmingham B5 6LB

Islamic Vision
481 Coventry Road
Birmingham B10 0JS

Jewish Care
221 Golders Green Road
London NW11

Jewish Education Bureau
8 Westcombe Avenue
Leeds LS8 2BS

Muslim Aid
PO Box 3
London N7 8LR

Muslim Educational Trust
130 Stroud Green Road
London N4 3RZ

Muslim Law (Shari'ah)
20–22 Creffield Road
London W5

Office of the Chief Rabbi
Adler House
Tavistock Square
London WC1H 9HN

Ramakrishna Vedanta Centre
Unity House
Blind Lane
Bourne End
Berkshire SL8 5LG

RSPCA
Causeway
Horsham
West Sussex RH12 1HG

Salvation Army Headquarters
101 Queen Victoria Street
London EC4P

The Swaminarayan Hindu Mission
Shri Swaminarayan Mandir
105–119 Brentfield Road
Neasden
London NW10 8SP

Tearfund
11 Station Road
Teddington
Middlesex TW11 9AA

Union of Liberal and Progressive Jews
Montague Centre
109 Westfield Street
London W1P 5RP

World Jewish Relief
Drayton House
30 Gordon Street
London WC1H 0AN

INDEX